Silver Screen Samurai

Published by DH Publishing, Inc.
Address: 2-3-3F Kanda Jimbocho, Chiyoda-ku, Tokyo 101-0051
Japan
www.dhp-online.com

cocoro books is an imprint of DH Publishing, Inc.

ISBN 0-9723124-3-9
Printed in Hong Kong

Printed by Miyuki Inter-Media Hong Kong Ltd.
Publisher: Hiroshi Yokoi
Publications Director: Clive Victor France
Design: Ichie Takahashi
Production: Takako Aoyama, Tomokazu Nagai, Tomoko Sakashita
Photography: Hidetoshi Shimazaki
Special thanks to Martin Foster, Rod Campbell, Satoshi Ikeda,
Tetsuya Masuda (@Wonder   www.atwonder.co.jp)

Contents

Features

Samurai Movie Posters
Intrigue, Betrayal, and Blood-cleansing

by Martin Foster

Martin Foster is a 26-year veteran of Japan, and once earned oodles of cash on very little sleep telling people where to invest their money. He now settles for less cash and more sleep as a freelance writer, and has developed a deep mistrust of financial analysts. He lists his hobbies as running, swimming, reading and receiving free movie tickets, but injury and age increasingly impact his performance in the more phsyical activities and he might have to cut back on the reading. His favorite samurai movie is Kagemusha.

Say what you will, the ultimate purpose of movie posters is to get bums on seats.

Employing a gamut of sales ploys still on display in the antics of bar touts, samurai movie posters persuade the customer to part with his hard-earned cash at the ticket window, and enter into the dark, moody world behind the curtain on the strength of implied promises of pleasure.

Although running an intense ticket-window battle with the Nikkatsu-powered pink subculture - the ultimate in tease, titillation, and killer taglines - the samurai movie was the dominant genre flooding onto wide screens well into the television period.

And it was typically lurid posters that promoted the moral tales of intrigue and betrayal, culminating in the penultimate sword-play that with a round of blood-cleansing vanquished evil and put society back on an even keel.

I do not pretend to be an expert in any of the specialized techniques associated with these posters. I am merely the kind of person who likes to see movies and believes my vast outlay of 1,800 yen per session gives me the right to call 'em as I see 'em...posters and all.

I have attempted to represent the names of actors and filmmakers mentioned in this introduction in western style - personal name followed by family name, and have included the English titles for the movies, whenever I've been able to find them.

 ## Simply Red

The first thing you notice about samurai posters is that they are big on the color red. As a result, there is a lot of red in this book, and none of it's medical or political. In most cases, it forms the major titles.

Running mostly top to bottom, and just at home on one side of the poster as on the other, the swathes of fire-engine red Chinese characters can also scream out their message in lateral mode - from either left to right or right to left. They may well be one of the more flexible elements of a samurai movie experience!

Apart from being designed to grab the attention, the use of the color may also be seen as a nod to the traditions of the samurai tale as told on-stage. In kabuki, certain colors represent the emotional state of a character, or are designed to provide insights into his or her motives.

Machibuse (1970)
Ambush

Not surprisingly red - deep red - is known as the color of anger, indignation, forceful-ness, and obstinacy.

All of these attitudes spring to mind when you come face to face with the guy with the mortar-board haircut and eye-splitting scar in the poster for **Tange Sazen**, who looks ready to realign your ears with his drawn sword.

The biggest splash of red on display in this book is a rough-cut swathe of brush-written characters for the 1970 movie **Machibuse** (**Ambush**). The main titles are so overpower-ing they have managed to shoulder-charge the players from center-stage.

Some of the most famous names in the genre appear in the movie, and the reason for the advent of the poster showing the all-star cast has been pinned on the need to have more dead bodies scattered around the screen to satisfy film-goers who had outgrown single star presentations with a death-count that could be totaled only on two hands!

Kumonosu-Jo (1957)
Throne of Blood

Let's be honest, for most people outside Japan, it is the combination of filmmaker Toshiro Mifune and Akira Kurosawa that defines the samurai movie genre in all its line 'em up and chop 'em down glory.

That relationship continued from *Yoidore Tenshi* (*Drunken Angel*) which Mifune starred in at the age of 28 in 1948, to *Akahige* (*Red Beard*) made in 1966. Mifune took best acting award at the Venice Film Festival three times, including for Akahige and **Yojimbo** in 1961.

However, while westerners consider Kurosawa to be the eastern director who influenced Hollywood directors from John Sturges to Stephen Spielberg, it is interesting to note that in Japan he is considered to be among the more western of Japanese directors.

A case in point is the 1957 movie **Kumonosu-Jo** (**Throne of Blood**), which Kurosawa loosely based on the tale of Macbeth. The movie was filmed on a set constructed on the lower levels of Mount Fuji, fully exploiting the desolate fog-shrouded backdrop to amplify the atmospherics in the scenes of madness and bloodletting.

(Am I seeing things, or is that music penned in around the edges of the posters for Kumonosu-Jo and **Joiuchi**?)

Zatoichi (2003)
Zatoichi

Mifune appears in approximately ten movies represented in this book but is outshone by another of his co-stars from Machibuse - Shintaro Katsu.

✿ Katsu Shin: The Sublime, the Ridiculous, and the Sad

Shintaro Katsu - who the Japanese, with their penchant for breaking down names and titles into easily chewable sizes, labeled Katsu Shin - appears in no less than 16 of the films covered in this book!

By the time of Machibuse he was already at the height of his popularity in his role as the blind masseur - Zatoichi. That series ran for a full 27 years from 1962 to 1989, and was reprised last year by Takeshi Kitano...complete with tap-dancing scene.

Before that, however, a totally bottom-line oriented move had seen the two huge stars of samurai movies share the spotlight and the split titles in the 1965 work - you guessed it - *Zatoichi to Yojimbo* (*Zatoichi meets Yojimbo*).

Goyokiba (1972)
Sword of Justice

Although one of the few on display that does not look like a freshly poured Bloody Mary, the poster for the 1957 film **Mori no Ishimatsu** - starring Katsu again - is equally garish; a green slash running left-to-right.

And Katsu is a busy man. His right arm menacingly raises a sword towards camera to complement his one-eyed glare. A restraining hand has been extended by the same actress that is purposely gripping Ishimatsu's breast. However, the grip is close to being a grope, and it's difficult to be sure what we are promised from this feature, especially as there is a shot of anger deep in her dark eyes and the very words on her pert lips seem to say - "How dare you!"

Still, the S&M tinted goings-on depicted on the poster for **Goyokiba** (**Sword of Justice**) and other antics of the "Hanzo the Razor" series starring Katsu - which only went to prove playing with swords wasn't the only thing on the mind of your average warrior - may just have been the kind of hanky-panky that spilled over into real life a little too often for the authorities in both Japan and the US.

Indeed, Katsu became the brunt of a round of bad jokes after being arrested in Hawaii attempting to leave the US with cocaine and marijuana hidden in his underwear. His son was arrested when an actor was killed with a real sword on the set of **Zatoichi**.

Semper Fi Mac, or That Loyalty "Thang"

The equally garish yellow lettering of **Teuchi** caps a mad-eyed Raizo Ichikawa, who looks set on revenge - possibly after being scalped.

The blurb on the right hand side of the page goes some way to explain the almost ecstatic expression on the face of the actress as she waits for the blow to fall. "A spectacle portraying the pathos of a man forced to kill the woman he loves. Is it because of the obstinacy of the warrior house, or a love grudge?"

Among the other 11 movies in this book that star Raizo Ichikawa - and where his name sometimes takes precedence over the likes of Katsu Shin - is **Shinsengumi Shimatsuki** (**Band of Assassins**). Along with the seemingly never-ending *Chushingura* and **Mito Komon**, Shinsengumi represents one of the stock samurai movie tales.

A paramilitary police force, the Shinsengumi terrorized and assassinated with virtual impunity in the imperial capital of Kyoto as it attempted to prop up the shogunate in its final days before the Meiji Restoration in 1868.

From the poster you'll be glad to know all that blood and gore comes in glorious "Natural Technicolor," and that the yellow blurb promotes the movie as an exposition of: "The loyalty of men which men love. The spirited young blood of the Shinsengumi."

Needless to say, the samurai code was big on loyalty with numerous variations on both the idea and the story rolled out throughout the history of the genre.

The poster for **Shinsengumi** promotes the 100th film appearance by Toshiro Mifune, and that old loyalty "thang" is in the catch copy: "Feared as a killing unit. They acted through their loyalty with the *katana*. The last samurai in Japan."

Shinsengumi (1969)
Shinsengumi

Taboo

With the poster for **Gohatto (Taboo)** director Nagisa Oshima presents us with an uncomfortable conundrum.

First, there is not a splash of red, or any other garish flag-striping to be seen anywhere. Then we have a simple title in both Chinese characters and Roman lettering printed in lavender with cast names below.

A single person stands alone in the center of the poster, instead of the "hundreds and thousands" seen in many over-populated posters that aimed to pack everything into a single promotion to draw the crowds.

Although the genre has gone off on a number of interesting tangents over the years, the typical protagonist of the samurai poster has been a wild-eyed, angry outcast, with a ministry of justice and revenge topped off with an outrageous mane of hair rivaled only by that of a certain modern-day Japanese prime minister. Yet, if he was nothing else in life, he was a man.

Sozaburo Kano is played by Ryuhei Matsuda, son of the late Yusaku Matsuda who appeared in **Hitogoroshi** and *Black Rain*. In the poster for Gohatto we are presented with a character whose lips harbor the suggestion of a pout, whose eyes are not so much rebellious as truculent, and whose hair looks as though it was coiffured at great cost by the same hairdresser who does the dos for the pneumatic Kano sisters.

His androgynous state is clearly designed to set off sexual tension.

Gohatto (1999)
Taboo

Gaba Gaba Hey?

Finally, if you like your posters to be mere accessories to the main event and to provide succinct, uncluttered, and mostly under-populated insights into the story line and never, ever take on a life of their own, this next poster is not for you.

The 1981 compilation film, **Chanbara Grafitti Kiru (The Chanbara Grafitti)** relives high-spots from approximately 100 well-known samurai movies made in the period from 1951 to 1960 in celebration of the 30th anniversary of the founding of Toei Studios.

And befitting a movie that runs the whole range of *chanbara* dramas, I count at least 18 figures on the poster. Only three have not drawn or are in the process of drawing arms; mainly Japanese swords, but one a conspicuous long-barreled pistol. Dirty Harry undercover in Japan?

The poster highlights its broad-based appeal: "Plaudits from the young. A thrill for the old. The days of glamorous period dramas are back!" And it does indeed appear to have something for every chanbara lover. Mito Komon is up front and at center.

While the smaller print reads just fine, it is the larger, red print that goes overboard: "Heroes. Villains. Assassins. Chop. Chop. Chopped! Dabadabada!"

I wonder if that should be translated: "Gaba Gaba Hey"?

Chanbara Graffiti Kiru! (1981)
The Chanbara Graffiti

Samurai Movie Posters
What to Look For

(1) Approximate value of poster/flyer
(2) Japanese title
(3) Year of production
(4) Studio
(5) English title*
(6) Director
(7) Leading actors
(8) Running time

(2)   (3)   (4)
Aru Kengo no Shogai (1959, Toho)
(5) ———— Life of a Swordsman
(6) ———— Hiroshi Inagaki
(7) ———— Toshiro Mifune, Yoko Tsukasa, Akira Takarada
(8) ———— 111 min

(1)
Poster (20 x 29 inch) $150.00

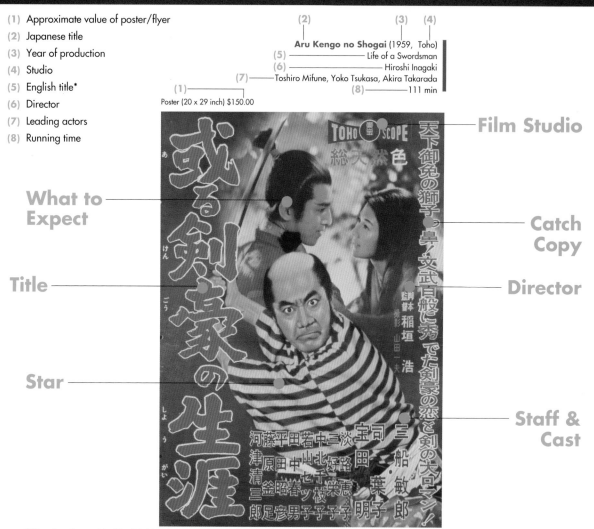

What to Expect

Title

Star

Film Studio

Catch Copy

Director

Staff & Cast

*When there is no original English title, an approximate translation has been given.

Glossary of terms used in this book

Bakufu the (Tokugawa) shogunate (government)

chanbara a sword fight; sword-play

Edo pre-1868 name of Tokyo (Edo period: 1603 - 1868)

daimyo a feudal lord

joruri the narrative which accompanies a Bunraku puppet show

kabuki a type of traditional Japanese drama which follows highly-stylized forms and takes up stories with popular appeal

kagemusha a double; a stand-in

kappa a water imp

kodachi a small, short sword

Kannon the Kannon; the Goddess of Mercy

onna kenshi a swordswoman

rakugo traditional comic storytelling

ronin a masterless samurai

seppuku ritual suicide (performed by samurai); hara-kiri

shamisen a samisen; a three-stringed Japanese banjo

Shogun a general; the Generalissimo

shogi Japanese chess

shuriken a throwing star or spike favored by ninja

1935~1959
昭和十年～昭和三十四年

Shinpen Tange Zazen (1935, Nikkatsu Kyoto)
Zazen Tange Returns
Sadao Yamanaka
Denjiro Okochi, Kiyozo, Kunitaro Sawamura
91 min

Poster (20 x 29 inch) $500.00

One of the many films featuring samurai superhero Zazen Tange, whose whopping scar across his right eye makes for an unforgettable image. When Tange creator Fubo Hayashi was invited to the movie's preview, he was aghast at the *rakugo* turn his story had taken, and complained to the film's maker Nikkatsu. Subsequently, the production was renamed *Zazen Tange Hearsay: The Priceless Pot* (although the poster says otherwise) and treated as a whole different story.

Poster (10 x 26 inch) $25.00

Shimizuko Daisan Yumedochu (1940, Nikkatsu Kyoto)
The Dream Road to Shimizu
Masahiro Makino
Chiezo Kataoka, Kunitaro Sawamura, Akio Sawamura
89 min

Genroku Abaregasa (1943, Toho)
The Angry Hat of Genroku
Tamizo Ishida
Ryunosuke Tsukigata, Kotaro Bando, Yataro Kurokawa

Poster (20 x 29 inch) $60.00

Stage director Ishida's anxiety over his upcoming play *Ishimatsu of Mori* is so acute that he awakes one morning to find that he's actually turned into Ishimatsu, the doomed mobster hero of the play's title. Ishida, fully aware of the legendary Ishimatsu's gruesome death, embarks on an adventure to change the future of his alter ego. For the day, the back-to-the-future plot was remarkably ahead of its time (pun not intended).

Yet another remake of the Chushingura raid of 47 *ronin* to avenge the death of their lord. Director Tamizo Ishida started at Toa Studios as an actor, but at the ripe old age of 23 he became the youngest Japanese director of his day. The man responsible for the film's wooden sandal-prints in the snow is none other than Eiji Tsuburaya, the creator of *Godzilla*.

Kessen Takadanobaba (1952, Toei Kyoto)
The Battle at Takadanobaba
Kunio Watanabe
Utaemon Ichikawa, Jun Tazaki, Nijiko Kiyokawa
98 min

Poster (16 x 19 inch) $25.00

Hero Yasubei Nakayama, who lives by his sword, is a favorite in his samurai neighborhood. But when his uncle is cut down in a duel, Yasubei sets out to reap revenge. The showdown takes place in Takadanobaba, now a Tokyo district famed as the birthplace of Astro Boy and revered by students for its cheap bars.

Nazo no Hissatsuken (1952, Shin Toho)
The Mysterious Blade
Nobuo Nakagawa
Kanjuro Arashi, Shigeru Ogura, Kingoro Yanagiya
88 min

Poster (20 x 29 inch) $100.00

When an actor is murdered on stage, samurai sleuth Umon Kondo, played here by Kanjuro Arashi, deduces that the culprit is from a rival theater. The film follows the efforts of this top-knotted Sherlock Holmes as he unravels the mystery and solves the case.

Kurama Tengu Kirikomu (1953, Takarazuka Eiga)
Kurama Tengu Attacks
Nobuo Adachi
Kanjuro Arashi, Michiyo Aratama, Danshiro Ichikawa

Poster (20 x 29 inch) $500.00

The 37th installment of Japan's most famous *chanbara* hero, Kurama Tengu. While Edo Castle is surrounded by government troops, a mysterious group called the Masakari Gumi takes advantage of the confusion to infiltrate and pillage in the name of the state. Kurama Tengu tags along to find out where their chief is hiding.

Hanazakari Otoko Ichidai (1955, Daiei Kyoto)
The Prime of Life
Kazuo Mori
Shintaro Katsu, Hiroko Yajima, Kunitaro Sawamura

Poster (20 x 29 inch) $80.00

Shintaro Katsu of *Zatoichi* fame plays a smitten mobster who takes up the *shamisen* to woo the woman he loves. But when she is kidnapped by an evil mafia boss, he exchanges his plectrum for a sword and embarks on a bloody rampage.

Poster (20 x 29 inch) $35.00

A period drama that borrows heavily from literary big gun Kodo Nomura's novel *Genjitsu Botenmaru*. A ghost has taken up residence at the Edo Palace. Has it been conjured by a mischievous sorcerer, or is it the work of Goro Bontenmaru, come to revenge the death of his father?

Poster (20 x 29 inch) $30.00

Since peace dawned across the land, the warriors that once fought under the banner of the Eighty-Thousand Knights have traded their heroics for lives of banditry. Daikichi Himura is one such crook, happy to spend his days robbing and looting. But when he's swindled by a beautiful woman all that changes, and so begins the action and adventure.

Orizuru Nana Henge (1956, Daiei Kyoto)
Seven Sides of the Folded Crane
Kimiyoshi Yasuda
Shintaro Katsu, Miyako Tachibana, Sumire Harukaze

Poster (20 x 29 inch) $50.00

An adventure story following sword-wielding twins and their quest to possess a mysterious folded paper crane. Shintaro Katsu is back, playing one of the brothers. Better known for his roles as villain, Katsu's art came back to haunt him when, at the age of 59, he was apprehended trying to board a plane in Hawaii with marijuana and cocaine stuffed down his underpants.

Yagyu Renyasai: Hiden Tsukikagesho (1956, Daiei Kyoto)
Renyasai Yagyu: The Secret Legend of the Moonlight Shadow
Katsuhiko Tasaka
Raizo Ichikawa, Shintaro Katsu, Yataro Kurokawa
84 min

Poster (20 x 29 inch) $45.00

A story of childhood friendship and adult rivalry that culminates in a testosterone-fueled slashfesh. Boyhood friends Tsunashiro Suzuki and Heisuke Yagyu study *mikiri*, an unassailable style of swordsmanship, under legendary bladesman Musashi Miyamoto. Eventually, the two fall out and a story of macho pride and intense rivalry unfolds. Adapted from the serialized novel by Yasuhiro Gomi.

Matashiro Kenka Tabi (1956, Daiei Kyoto)
Matashiro's Travels
Katsuhiko Tasaka
Raizo Ichikawa, Michiko Saga, Tokiko Mita
85 min

Poster (20 x 29 inch) $100.00

The story of two princesses, heirs to the House of Suwa, and the power struggles that rage around them. When one leaves for Edo, her enemies plot do her in along the way. But into the action jumps the film's hero, Matashiro Sasai, who time and again saves her from the murderous schemes that have been hatched against her. As it so often does after near-death experiences, love blossoms between the two.

Mori no Ishimatsu (1957, Daiei Kyoto)
Ishimatsu of Mori
Katsuhiko Tasaka
Shintaro Katsu, Michiko Ono, Michiko Ai
87 min

Poster (20 x 29 inch) $80.00

Yakuza Ishimatsu of Mori dines with a stranger, little knowing that he is the famous boss Jirocho of Shimizu. Ishimatsu eventually becomes his retainer, but while Jirocho is away, Ishimatsu goes AWOL and opens a gambling den under his boss' name. The conclusion is a violent fracas with members of a rival gang.

Poster (20 x 29 inch) $60.00

Shakespeare's *Macbeth* reset in the Era of Warring States. Power-hungry Taketoki Washizu becomes lord of Kumonosu Castle after murdering his master Kuniharu. Accused of the crime, Noriyasu, the famed military tactician and warlord of the neighboring state, rustles up an army and invades.

Nobushi to Onna (1957, Shochiku Kyoto)
The Warriors and the Lady
Tatsuo Sakai
Sadaji Takahashi, Mieko Takamine, Hiroshi Nawa

Poster (20 x 29 inch) $22.00

Two young samurai in the service of Toyotomi, Koyata Matsumae and Hikosaku Amamori have given up any hope of surviving the war when they come across an enemy princess. This sets them thinking about how they may make the most of the situation. But each has his own plan, which leads to rivalry and ultimately swords are unsheathed.

Tabi wa Kimagure Kazemakase (1958, Daiei Kyoto)
Let the Wind Guide You
Katsuhiko Tasaka
Raizo Ichikawa, Jun Negami, Yoko Uraji
79 min

Poster (20 x 29 inch) $40.00

Genta, the son of a conjurer and samurai descendant, and Sanji, the second son of a mafia boss, have both run away from home to seek adventure. They meet by chance at a teashop and immediately hit it off. With sleight of hand, they win big at a gambling den and are all set to enjoy their riches. But their cheating doesn't go unnoticed, and the story comes alive as they try to escape the wrath of their fellow gamblers.

Benten Kozo (1958, Daiei Kyoto)
Benten Kozo
Daisuke Ito
Raizo Ichikawa, Kyoko Aoyama, Michiko Ai
86 min

Poster (20 x 29 inch) $60.00

A *rakugo* period drama that takes a kabuki play as its theme. The story is by Mokuami Kawatake, known to many as Japan's Shakespeare. Benten Kozo and his gang of yakuza save a young woman from an attack. However, far from good Samaritans, they intend to sell her into slavery. But Benten has a heart, and, charmed by the girl's innocence, he decides to rescue her from her rescuers.

Silver Screen Samurai Legends

Denjiro Okochi
(1898 -1962)

Denjiro Okochi studied drama with the ambition of becoming a playwright before joining Nikkatsu Studios in 1926. His break came in the following year, when his performance in the trilogy *Chuji Tabi Nikki* caught the eye of director Daisuke Ito. With his commanding looks, theatrical eloquence and an abundance of energy, he quickly became an audience favorite. But it was the role of Tange Zazen, which he famously pronounced "Jajen", that secured his place as an on-screen great. In 1936, he moved to Toho Studios, and then on to Shin Toho, Daiei and finally Toei. Okochi was a keen gardener, and his mountain villa is now a designated "Important Cultural Site".

Star Performance
Tange Zazen
Recommended Viewing - Okochi's 13-film Tange Zazen series; Daibosatsu Toge (1957); Kobo Shinsengumi (1930)

Tsumasaburo Bando
(1901 - 1953)

Discovered in 1923 by director Masahiro Makino, Tsumasaburo Bando soon made the shift from kabuki stage to film set, bringing to his period dramas a realism that, after the release of *Kageboshi* in 1925, would catapult him to almost immediate stardom. Affectionately known as "Bantsuma", in 1925 he became the first actor in Japan to establish his own production company. But with the commencement of talkies, his fans, who had cheered him through his silent pictures, were startled by his surprisingly high-pitched voice, and his career seemed doomed. The 1937 release of *Koiyamabiko*, however, put him back on top.

Star Performance
Matsugoro Tomishima
Recommended Viewing - Senketsu no Tegata (1923); Orochi (1925); Muhomatsu no Issho (1943)

Ryunosuke Tsukigata
(1902 - 1970)

One of the early graduates of Japan's first acting school, Ryunosuke Tsukigata endured years of poverty before his role alongside Tsumasaburo Bando in *Utaruru Mono* (1924) launched his film career. He excelled in second lead or villain roles, acquiring a huge following among a younger generation of movie-goers. Even as his fame eclipsed his fellow stars, he continued to accept secondary roles. He never lost sight of his humble beginnings, and worked hard to improve the lot of the professional actor.

Star Performance   Mito Komon
Recommended Viewing - Miyamoto Musashi (1940); Tateshi Danpei (1950); Oborokago (1951)

Chiezo Kataoka
(1903 - 1983)

As a kabuki child prodigy, Chiezo Kataoka expected to continue his career in the theater. However, in adulthood, he found the austere regime of kabuki to be unbearable, and reinvented himself as a movie actor, making his debut in the 1923 picture *Sanshiku Sumire*. He quickly became a star of the period drama genre, going on to form his own company Chiezo Production. With upcoming directors Hiroshi Ingaki and Mansaku Itami in tow, he went on to make one hit after another. Although a dedicated follower of the samurai drama, he willingly attempted contemporary themes, to which he brought his unique sense of presence. One of the founding members of Toei Studios, Kataoka is remembered as a star of the golden age of period dramas.

Star Performance   Bannai Tarao
Recommended Viewing - Mabuta no Haha (1931); Ippongatana Doyoiri (1931); Akanishi Kakita (1936)

Kanjuro Arashi
(1903 - 1980)

"Arakan", as he became known to his many fans, was one of the first Japanese actors to reach nationwide stardom. His inimitable style, which even today seems remarkably innovative, appealed to young and old alike. Not limited to playing samurai, two of his most memorable roles were Emma, King of Hades and the Emperor of Japan. By the end of his career, he had appeared in over 330 movies. Kanjuro Arashi's life off camera was just as colorful. Much of his wealth he lost to gambling and the four women he married and divorced in succession.

Star Performance
Kurama Tengu, Muttsuri Umon
Recommended Viewing - 30-film Kurama Tengu series; 34-film Umon Torimonocho; Karakuri Cho (1929)

Stars of Japan's Golden Age of Cinema

Utaemon Ichikawa
(1907 - 1999)

Utaemon Ichikawa's early fascination with drama led him to join the Kansai kabuki troupe, where he quickly rose to fame. However, he found it difficult to win lead roles in a world dominated by family lineage. By chance, he was spotted by director Shozo Makino, who persuaded him to seek a career in film. He made his lead debut in the 1925 movie *Kurogami Jigoku*, but it was the release of *Hatamoto Taikutsu Otoko* that cemented his fame.

Star Performance   Mondonosuke Saotome
Recommended Viewing - Hatamoto Taikutsu Otoko series

Ryutaro Otomo
(1912 - 1985)

Alongside Chiezo Kataoka and Utaemon Ichikawa, Ryutaro Otomo is recognized as one of the greats of the golden age of Toei period dramas. Although best known for the rough, plain-talking characters he played, he was a remarkably flexible actor, coupling his film work with a successful career on stage. In later years, he even moved into television. Otomo is remembered for his roles as Kaiketsu Kurozukin, Tange Zazen and, more recently, as the noodle master in Juzo Itami's acclaimed movie *Tanpopo* (1985).

Star Performance
Kaiketsu Kurozukin, Tange Zazen
Recommended Viewing - 8-film Kaiketsu Kurozukin series; Otomo's 5-film Tange Zazen series; Kaiketsu Maboroshizukin (1954)

Chiyonosuke Azuma
(1926 - 2000)

Chiyonosuke Azuma took up Japanese dance (*nihonbuyo*) at the age of 19, which led to a career as a kabuki dance coach. In 1954, he auditioned for a part as a young dancer at Toei Studios and made his screen debut in the box office hit *Yukinojo Henge*. He soon teamed up with Kinnosuke Nakamura (later to become Kinnosuke Yorozuya), who had made the transition from stage to film at the same time. The duo garnered an immediate following among movie-goers, who revelled in the contrast between the unrefined Nakamura and Azuma, who cut a dashing figure with his handsome looks and elegant manners.

Star Performance
Hagimaru
Recommended Viewing - Fuefuki Doji (1954); Beni Kujaku (1954); Satomi Hakkenden (1954);

Hashizo Okawa
(1929 - 1984)

After a successful early career as a bewitching *onnagata* (female-role actor in kabuki), Hashizo Okawa joined Toei Studios in 1955. He quickly rose in his new profession. Although he returned to the stage when, in the mid-60s, Toei fortunes slumped, he also moved into television. From 1966 to 1984, he starred in the much-loved TV series *Zenigata Heiji*, making 888 appearances, a record for a one-hour TV series now listed in the Guinness Book of Records.

Star Performance
Heiji Zenigata
Recommended Viewing - Shingo Juban (1959); Wakasama Samurai Torimonocho (1956); Odeiri (1964)

Raizo Ichikawa
(1931 -1969)

Raizo Ichikawa gained a huge following after making his screen debut in the 1954 film *Hana no Byakkotai*. Although in real life outgoing and cheerful, he is remembered most for the extraordinarily dark characters that he played on film. In his short career, which ended with his death at 37 from illness, he appeared in over 150 movies that dealt with themes from samurai stories to literary works to modern drama.

Star Performance
Nemuri Kyoshiro
Recommended Viewing - Nemuri Kyoshiro series; Shin-Heike Monogatari (1955); Shinobi no Mono (1962)

Shichinin Wakashu Tanjo (1958, Shochiku Kyoto)
Band of Seven
Ryosuke Kurahashi
Kinshiro Matsumoto, Kotobuki Hananomoto, Hitoe Otani

Poster (20 x 29 inch) $30.00

Seven temple boys escape to live hidden in Koya Mountain. Each carries with him memories of a dark past. The movie introduces seven newcomers, including Yoichi Hayashi and Kotobuki Hananomoto.

Tokaido no Yarodomo (1958, Daiei Kyoto)
The Lads of Tokaido
Katsuhiko Tasaka
Shintaro Katsu, Michiko Ono, Michiko Ai

Poster (20 x 29 inch) $50.00

A comedy starring the ubiquitous Shintaro Katsu. Hanji lives to gamble, fight and sing and believes his life will be of little else. But as the story unfolds, he becomes husband, son-in-law and relative, and soon his troubles really begin.

Yagyu Bugeicho: Soryu Hiken (1958, Toho)
The Book of Yagyu: Double Dragon Sword
Hiroshi Inagaki
Koji Tsuruta, Toshiro Mifune, Nobuko Otowa
106 min

Poster (20 x 29 inch) $100.00

More than the fate of Tokugawa hangs in the balance. The secrets of the *Book of Yagyu* threaten to bring down the Imperial Household itself. In a sword-wielding free-for-all, an array of characters are out to get their hands on it, including the evil Yagyu Clan, ninja, and the Komuso Gang. Senshiro, a ninja caught up in the chase, saves a beautiful princess from the hands of Jubei Yagyu. But it turns out she is also seeking the fateful tome...

Abare Daimyo (1959, Toei Kyoto)
The Rowdy Daimyo
Kokichi Uchide
Utaemon Ichikawa, Keiko Okawa, Kogiku Hanayagi
90 min

Poster (20 x 29 inch) $35.00

Set in the early days of the Ieyasu Tokugawa government. Keijiro is the spirited nephew of Toshiie Maeda, the feudal lord of Kaga-han, whose only desire is to suck up to the new ruling elite. To help his uncle succeed, Keijiro comes up with the brilliant plan of returning the samurai's payment to the government. However, another evil daimyo has plans to take advantage of the young man's enthusiasm. In the end, all is revealed.

Aru Kengo no Shogai (1959, Toho)
Life of a Swordsman
Hiroshi Inagaki
Toshiro Mifune, Yoko Tsukasa, Akira Takarada
111 min

Poster (20 x 29 inch) $150.00

Chiyoda-Jo Enjo (1959, Daiei Kyoto)
Fire at Chiyoda Castle
Kimiyoshi Yasuda
Michiyo Aratama, Shintaro Katsu, Tokiko Mita

Poster (20 x 29 inch) $50.00

A samuraization of the Edmond Rostard classic *Cyrano de Bergerac*. The lead character is played by snouty Toshiro Mifune, an excellent choice for the part of a kind and serious man who, unlucky in love, channels his energies into the mastery of swordsmanship.

Chizuru, a poor girl, leaves her sick father and her lover to start life as a maid at the palace. Although once there she is mistreated by all around her, she sets out to navigate the power struggles of the servants' quarter and succeed in her new career. With her promotion comes enemies, and one day a jealous servant sets fire to her room. The blaze is brought under control, and Chizuru's career gets a lift. Soon she is ruler of her domain, but still she remains unsatisfied.

Bakumatsu Bishonenroku: Aizu no Kesshitai (1959, Toei Kyoto)
Boys in the Last Days of Bakufu: Aizu's Suicide Corps
Masamitsu Igayama
Kotaro Satomi, Hiromi Hanazono, Seishiro Sawamura
63 min

Poster (20 x 29 inch) $35.00

It is the twilight years of Bakufu rule and the seemingly invincible government forces are marching on Aizu-han. The castle will not withstand another attack. The troops are dead or have fled leaving only women and children. The Aizu Suicide Corps, a band of old men not fit to fight and boys too young to become samurai, are the last defense. None of them expects to survive...

Chiyari Muso (1959, Toei Kyoto)
The Bloody Lance
Yasushi Sasaki
Chiezo Kataoka, Hashizo Okawa, Tomisaburo Wakayama
99 min

Poster (20 x 29 inch) $30.00

Takuminokami Asano grows angry at Kozukenosuke Kira's abuse and draws his sword, committing a samurai faux pas. To absolve himself, he slices open his own stomach and by doing so ends the Asano family lineage. Asano's followers, known as Ako Roshi and led by Kuranosuke Oishi, are pissed, and swear to revenge their dead master.

Haruna Bayashi: Kenkadaka (1959, Toei Kyoto)
Haruna Festival Music
Kokichi Uchide
Utaemon Ichikawa, Kinya Kitaoji, Keiko Okawa
84 min

Poster (20 x 29 inch) $25.00

A story of yakuza honor and duty. Shinsuke owes Torakichi Otaya for feeding and clothing him. As a way to repay his kind-ness, Shinsuke cuts down Torakichi rival Tomogoro. To hide out until the heat is off, Shinsuke leaves his girl, Shizuha, at home and disappears. Torakichi, meanwhile, decides to try it on with Shizuha, who's not having any of it. Eventually, Shinzuke learns of Torakichi's deviousness and returns for the necessary revenge.

Poster (20 x 29 inch) $35.00

Another detective story cum slashfest, this time revolving around the illustrious Kido samurai family. Shinnosuke, a descendent of Seiwa Genji, is murdered. His follower Genzaburo suspects the culprits are after the family fortune, and goes forth to uncover the plot and revenge his master's death. This he finally does, appearing before his enemies disguised as the murdered Shinnosuke.

Machibugyo Nikki: Tekkabotan (1959, Daiei Kyoto)
The Diaries of a Town Magistrate: A High-spirited Woman
Kenji Misumi
Shintaro Katsu, Keiko Awaji, Jun Negami
90 min

Poster (20 x 29 inch) $30.00

Screen adaptation of the novel by Shugoro Yamamoto, who now has a literary award named after him. Kenji Misumi, the director of this period comedy, is better known for his classic Japanese horror movie *Yotsuya Kaidan*.

O'oka Seidan: Chidori no Inro (1959, Toei Kyoto)
The Politics of O'oka: The Plover Pillbox
Yasushi Sasaki
Chiezo Kataoka, Keiko Okawa, Chizuru Kitagawa
79 min

Poster (20 x 29 inch) $60.00

A dramatization of the period detective novel *The Legend of Satomi's Eight Dogs (Satomi Hakken Den)*. One evening, Hankuro Mizuki, a cop at the Minamicho Magistrates Court, witnesses a young woman throw herself into Sumida River. But also watching calmly from nearby are members of the Black Mask Gang, who row out in a small boat and pluck her from the water before she can drown. Gumshoe Mizuki decides to investigate, and follows the gang as they disappear into the night. But before he can get very far, he is set upon. Who are these masked men, and what evil plans are they hatching...?

Seki no Yatappe (1959, Daiei Kyoto)
Yatappe of Seki
Bin Kato
Kazuo Hasegawa, Shintaro Katsu, Tamao Nakamura
82 min

Poster (20 x 29 inch) $100.00

A period yakuza flick starring Kazuo Hasegawa. Yakuza Yataro from the town of Seki is out minding his own business when a man approaches with a girl and suddenly jumps him. During the struggle, the stranger foolishly stabs himself in the stomach, and Yataro is stuck with the girl. He quickly dumps her with her nearest living relatives and departs. 10 years pass, and the girl grows up to be a beautiful young woman, which, in the scheme of things, makes her a prime target for attack. However, just when her virtue looks set to be compromised, in steps Yataro again to save the day. The girl has a flashback, remembering the good yakuza from times passed. But Yataro is all grace and modesty. He denies that they have ever met, and the two part, never to meet again.

Tenryu no Karasu (1959, Daiei Kyoto)
The Crow of Tenryu
Kimiyoshi Yasuda
Shintaro Katsu, Shoji Umewaka, Joji Tsurumi

Poster (20 x 29 inch) $60.00

Shintaro Katsu reappears as Kantaro from Tenryu. Vicious gang boss Komazo bumps off a government official and pins the blame on Kantaro. But an eyewitness to the murder surfaces and it's none other than Ginji, whose life Kantaro once saved. After Ginji blabbers, Kantaro is exonerated and all live happily ever after.

Utagoyomi Shusse Sugoroku (1959, Toei Kyoto)
Utagoyomi: The Fortunes of a Minstrel
Daisuke Yamazaki
Kotaro Satomi, Keiko Okawa, Hiromi Hanazono
69 min

Poster (20 x 29 inch) $28.00

Kotaro Satomi of long-running TV period drama *Mito Komon* fame stars in this samurai musical. Minstrel Choji and his backing band fall into debt with a wicked moneylender who demands his pound of flesh. The showdown coincides with a parade of the region's feudal lords. Just as Choji looks set to meet his maker, a young lord, bored of the festivities, comes to the rescue.

1960~1969
昭和三十五年～昭和四十四年

Echigo Shishi Matsuri (1960, Shochiku Kyoto)
Echigo Lion Dance Festival
Kunio Watanabe
Takahiro Tamura, Michiko Saga, Kyoko Kawaguchi
88 min

Poster (20 x 29 inch) $25.00

Various events conspire to entice Hanjiro of Katakai to a festival with a troupe of performers he has recently met. Shinemon Echigoya, the rice wholesaler who invited the troupe, realizes from Hanjiro's amulet that he is his very own son who he was forced to sell long ago. But Hanjiro, unimpressed, denies that he ever had parents.

Daitengu Shutsugen (1960, Shin Toho)
Daitengu Comes to Life
Masaki Mori
Kanjuro Arashi, Kotaro Bando, Shozaburo Date
81 min

Poster (20 x 29 inch) $150.00

Set in the turbulent days of the Bakufu government as Japan's centuries-long self-imposed isolation is nearing its end. Shogun councilor Yamatonokami Kuze and Brennan, an advisor to American Consulate General Townsend Harris, concoct a plan to smuggle in ammunition and make a killing, figuratively speaking. But their plans are foiled by the self-styled action hero "Shimoda Daitengu", whose disguise is replete with white kimono topped with bright red Tengu mask.

Kuroshio Hibun: Jigoku no Hyakuman Ryo (1960, Shochiku Kyoto)
Kuroshio Hibun: The Wages of Hell
Ryo Hagiwara
Masakazu Tamura, Shoji Yasui, Miki Mori
81 min

Poster (20 x 29 inch) $25.00

The powerful and wicked Echizennokami Mizuno, Kainokami Torii and their followers sweep across the land murdering with indifference. Genzaburo is particularly unlucky: His foster father is killed and his sweetheart dragged away screaming. He swears vengeance and disappears to the far-off kingdom of Ryukyu, today's Okinawa. Years later, dispatched as a messenger of the king, Genzaburo hides his identity and returns to Nagasaki to take revenge.

Kizu Sen Ryo (1960, Daiei Kyoto)
The Priceless Wound
Tokuzo Tanaka
Kazuo Hasegawa, Kyoko Kagawa, Keiko Yumi
103 min

Poster (20 x 29 inch) $30.00

Dramatization of Shin Hasegawa's famed novel *Kizu Takakura*. Close friends, Cho'uemon Takakura and Mohei Togo live alongside each other in the Aizu-han region. However, one day they fall into an argument, and decide to settle it with swords. In a fight to the death, Cho'uemon comes out victorious. Mohei's brother Matahachiro, seething with anger, vows to revenge his sibling's death. But it turns out that his wife Suga was once Cho'uemon's servant and secretly the girl of his dreams.

Nijinosuke Midare Katana (1960, Daiei Kyoto)
Nijinosuke's Flashing Sword
Masateru Nishiyama
Yutaka Nakamura, Ryuzo Shimada, Joji Tsurumi

Poster (20 x 29 inch) $20.00

Nijinosuke Omokage makes a good living by fighting. So he's not too happy when a lady fighter going by the name of Yuminosuke Yano sets herself up as a business rival. However, he learns that, together with her sister, her true aim is to find her father's killer. Nijinosuke is impressed, and decides to do all he can to help the girls.

Shogi Daimyo Dokuro Hen, Maboroshi Hen (1960, Daini Toei Kyoto)
The Shogi Daimyo
Hideaki Ohnishi
Sentaro Fushimi, Eiko Maruyama, Atsuko Nakazato

Poster (20 x 29 inch) $20.00

A detective samurai story based on two volumes, *The Skull* and *The Phantom*. In an Edo town, a gruesome murder has taken place. The *shuriken* used to kill the victim has attached to it a diagram of a *shogi* move. The game has flourished under the Bakufu government and shogi halls abound. At one of these works So'in Ito, whose interest in the murder and the shogi puzzle leads him to investigate.

Teki wa Honnoji ni Ari (1960, Shochiku Kyoto)
The Enemy at Honno Temple
Tatsuo Osone
Koshiro Matsumoto, Takahiro Tamura, Michiko Saga

Poster (20 x 29 inch) $25.00

Screenplay by Naoki Award-winner Shotaro Ikenami and based on historical events. The story takes place during the Era of Warring States, when Nobunaga Oda was fighting to unify Japan. Mitsuhide Akechi, a charismatic Nobunaga vassal, grows to despise his master's lies and treachery and plots to bring down the great leader. This he does, by murdering Nobunaga and subsequently making history. But his victory is short-lived. 11 days later, he is slain by another Nobunaga vassal Hideyoshi Hashiba.

Furisode Kosho Torimonocho: Chimonjihada (1961, Toei Kyoto)
The Boy in the Long-sleeved Kimono: Written on Skin
Kinnosuke Fukada
Tossho Sawamura, Atsuko Nakazato, Akemi Misawa

Poster (20 x 29 inch) $30.00

The entire Minoya family is mysteriously slaughtered. The only clue is the character for red - or *aka* - carved into the breast of the daughter Oshino. Furthermore, a girl has gone missing from town, and when her corpse is found the same character has been carved onto her body. When Gennosuke Fue, a palace page, hears of the murders, he knows that something ain't right. He heads to the Edo Castle library to do some reading-up, and comes across the story of the Shumon (Red Crest) Clan...

Poster (20 x 29 inch) $70.00

Although brothers from a good samurai family, Shinnosuke, the elder brother played by Raizo Ichikawa, and his younger sibling Shinjiro, played by Yukio Hashi, are like chalk and cheese. Shinnosuke is prim and proper; Shinjiro is a been-there-done-that yakuza. But when their father is killed, they must join forces to revenge his death. The result is a hilarious buddy-samurai flick that garnered a big male following.

Kengo Tengu Matsuri (1961, Toei Kyoto)
Swordsman at the Tengu Festival
Shigehiro Ozawa
Ryutaro Otomo, Eiji Okada, Keiko Okawa
87 min

Poster (20 x 29 inch) $25.00

Master swordsman Shirogoro Bushi travels to Edo to compete in the Imperial Sword-fighting Tournament. The contest goes well, and he looks set to easily win. However, to his surprise, the judges rule against him. It is a rude awakening. He realizes that, as in the world of politics, the swordsman's world is also one of corruption and greed. He leaves the capital disheartened and heads for home. But on his way he meets Isohime, and together they set off for the mountains of Aizu.

Kojiro Tsubame-gaeshi (1961, Daiei Kyoto)
Kojiro and Tsubame-gaeshi
Katsuhiko Tasaka
Shintaro Katsu, Tamao Nakamura, Hideo Takamatsu

Poster (20 x 29 inch) $50.00

Based on the true story of swordsman Kojiro Sasaki, who perfected the famed sword strike Tsubame-gaeshi (Swallow Counter). Sasaki becomes an apprentice of *kodachi* master Seigen Tomita, but must battle his teacher's enemies as part of the curriculum. He comes to realize the complexities of swordsmanship and the need to resist all distraction. He finally masters his lessons and through this perfects the sword strike that would lend its name, among other things, to moves in judo and in video games, a sex position and a brand of *sake*.

Kirimaru Kirigakure: Nankai no Okami (1961, Toei Kyoto)
Kirimaru, The Man of the Mist: South Sea Wolf
Shoji Matsumura
Hiroki Matsukata, Hiromi Hanazono, Hiroko Yoshikawa
88 min

Poster (20 x 29 inch) $20.00

The second of the *Kirimaru* series released in the same year. In the first film, the story revolves around the search for treasure hidden in the Black Kannon statue and Kirimaru's narrow escape with his girlfriend Namie from their dastardly foes. In this one, Namie's back in trouble, after getting snatched by an evil gang hot in search of the treasure. Kirimaru sets out to rescue his sweetheart and falls in with a band of pirates also hunting the hidden stash.

Matashiro Gyojoki: Shinpen Bijo Komori (1961, Toei Kyoto)
Matashiro's Stories of Conduct: Mystery of the Bat Woman
Toshikazu Kono
Koji Takada, Tomisaburo Wakayama, Hiroko Sakuramachi

Poster (20 x 29 inch) $80.00

Ronin Matashiro Sasai saves geisha girl Otsuya from being kidnapped by a gang of lawless samurai, and by doing so learns of a feud between two princesses in the Iwakitaira region. One princess is set to marry into the local aristocracy. But an evil retainer in Edo hopes to use poor Otsuya to snatch the official register of ancestry and upset the wedding plans. Although two different screenplays, both this story and *Matashiro's Travels* are adaptations of the same book.

Oani'isan to On'e'esan (1961, Daiei Kyoto)
Big Brother, Big Sister
Yoshiyuki Kuroda
Shintaro Katsu, Masayo Banri, Katsuhiko Kobayashi

Poster (20 x 29 inch) $40.00

Both gypsy Sanjiro and yakuza Hachigoro have got the hots for the same girl, Osen, whose uncle Senuemon just happens to be a gangster. So when it looks as if she'll be taken away against her will, they step in to save her. However, not long after, Hachigoro decides to bump off Senuemon, leaving Osen more than a little peeved. Hachigoro swears revenge, but is persuaded to seek justice through the law.

Onna to San Akunin (1961, Toei Kyoto)
One Woman, Three Bad Men
Umetsugu Inoue
Fujiko Yamamoto, Shintaro Katsu, Tamao Nakamura
102 min

Poster (20 x 29 inch) $100.00

A period drama with a comical slant written and directed by Umetsugu Inoue. The ubiquitous Shintaro Katsu plays disastrous husband to Tamao Nakamura's long-suffering wife. The couple somehow manages to survive a tumultuous marriage, and it takes the death of the husband to finally tear them apart.

Owari no Abarejishi (1961, Toei Kyoto)
Crazy Lion
Toshikazu Kono
Ryutaro Otomo, Satomi Oka, Sumiko Hidaka
86 min

Poster (20 x 29 inch) $30.00

The story takes place under the rule of General Hachidai. Two Tokugawa regions, Owari and Kishu, are sworn enemies. Owari's young lord, Mangoro, is a rather unconventional character who has earned the nickname Crazy Lion. In an effort to bring down their foe, the Kishus spy on the Owaris and soon discover through stolen building plans that the Owaris are refortifying their castle. This goes against shogunate law, and the Kishus lose no time in snitching to the government.

Poster (20 x 29 inch) $25.00

Hyosuke Katsuragi, second son of a retainer at the shogun's castle, is a drunk and spendthrift. Senshiro Matsudaira is a cheap-skate with a penchant for sweets. The two are constantly arguing over the most trivial matters. In step a local liquor merchant and a feudal lord, both looking for future husbands for their daughters. All four young people refuse to have anything to do with each other. This leads to high jinx and easy laughs as one comical situation unfolds into another until finally all comes happily together.

Oyakusha Henge Torimonocho: Chidokuro Yashiki (1961, New Toei Kyoto)
The Mystery of the Actor: Bloody Skull Mansion
Toshikazu Kono
Kokiti Takada, Keiko Okawa, Keiko Ogimachi

Poster (20 x 29 inch) $30.00

The sign outside Ippei Kasumi's general store reads, "Whatever you need to know, whatever you want done". One day, gambler Sangoro charges into the shop crying he has escaped kidnap by a band of mysterious samurai. Ippei learns from Sangoro's sister about the strange goings-on at the Goto residence, where she works as a maid. He puts two and two together and realizes the bad guys must be destroyed. This he does by joining forces with famed actor Kikunojo, of whom he is a spitting image, and foiling his evil foe.

Wakatono Senryohada (1961, Toei Kyoto)
The Lordly Actor
Kosaku Yamashita
Tossho Sawamura, Tomisaburo Wakayama, Kyoji Sugi
65 min

Poster (20 x 29 inch) $15.00

The first film by famed yakuza movie director Kosaku Yamashita. To expose the smuggling operations of fat cat royal retainer Shuzen Hirayama, the young lord Kiritaro Inaba disguises himself as a *ronin* and goes forth.

Abekobe Dochu (1962, Toei Kyoto)
On the Wrong Road
Toshikazu Kono
Chiyonosuke Higashi, Shingo Yamashiro, Isao Yamagata
65 min

Poster (20 x 29 inch) $30.00

A villager, who poses as a famous and learned palace teacher, comes across a young girl in trouble. He rescues her only to find that she's actually daughter of the mighty Iga Family. They confront each other, for although he claims to be a great man, she has never heard of him. He finally persuades her that he's the real thing. But by that time he has fallen for her and, no longer able to keep up the pretense, he disappears forever.

Hachiman Hatokuro (1962, Toei Kyoto)
Hatokuro Hachiman
Shoji Matsumura
Kokichi Takada, Kotaro Satomi, Hiroko Sakuramachi
86 min

Poster (20 x 29 inch) $20.00

Shogun Councilor Sadanobu Matsudaira discovers that to oppose the corruption of the government by fellow councilor and arch villain Okitsugu Tanuma is dangerous indeed. One by one, Matsudaira's comrades are disposed of by the murderous Murasaki Gang. To uncover the wicked deeds, detective Shinkichi of Tamaya joins forces with elegant *ronin* Hatokuro Hachiman.

Hana to Yato no Mure (1962, Toei Kyoto)
Flowers and Mobs
Shigehiro Ozawa
Hiroki Matsukata, Yoshihisa Hojo, Sayuri Tachikawa
89 min

Poster (20 x 29 inch) $20.00

Young bandit Tarobo of Minamoto, who likes to think of himself as the son of legendary thief Goemon Ishikawa, rampages through the countryside of Sagano with impunity. However, he has one weakness. Since his affair with Orin, the daughter of another bandit, he dreams of one thing only - to become top dog of her father's gang.

Mukomizu no Kenkagasa (1962, Toei Kyoto)
The Reckless Fighting Hat
Daisuke Yamazaki
Kotaro Satomi, Shingo Yamashiro, Michiko Nishizaki
77 min

Poster (20 x 29 inch) $25.00

Nagadosu Chushingura (1962, Daiei Kyoto)
Long Daggers of Chushingura
Kunio Watanabe
Raizo Ichikawa, Kojiro Hongo, Shintaro Katsu
97 min

Poster (20 x 29 inch) $100.00

Sataro of Haruna, whose rain hat makes him look like a *kappa*, helps pretty Okimi out during a scuffle on the road to Nikko. However, while delivering the beautiful white horse Shirayuki to a temple as an offering, Okimi again comes under attack, this time by the bosses of the posting station, the Aragami Clan. She is taken prisoner, but Sataro soon comes to the rescue.

The setting is the period that presaged the fall of the Tokugawa shogunate. A yakuza boss is attempting to preserve the lifestyles of the local farmers and townsfolk, but is picked up on some trumped up charge and executed by the lord of Hamamatsu Castle. *Long Daggers* is a yakuza version of the well-known Chushingura story, and tells of how some 40 yakuza retainers take a stand to avenge their master's murder.

もはや、敵なし。

北野武 監督作品
ビートたけし 主演

座頭市

a film by Takeshi Kitano "ZATOICHI"
http://www.office-kitano.co.jp/zatoichi/
2003年9月ロードショー

Zatoichi - The Blind Masseur and the Screen Legend

Zatoichi (2003, Bandai Visual, Tokyo FM, Dentsu, Asahi National Broadcasting, Saito Entertainment, Office Kitano)
Director: Takeshi Kitano
115 min

Takeshi Kitano's 2003 movie *Zatoichi* took four awards at the 60th Venice International Film Festival, including that for best director. The film went on to win international acclaim, but in Japan no one doubted that its success owed much to the star of the original *Zatoichi* series - Shintaro Katsu.

For the Japanese, *Zatoichi* and Shintaro Katsu are as inseparable as cherry blossom and spring. Takeshi Kitano underscored this when first offered the part. He turned it down, claiming that in his opinion no one else could ever play the famed blind masseur. It was only when he was offered the roles of director, producer and lead in a film that would only need retain the title and basic Zatoichi ingredients that he yielded to the temptation to rework this masterpiece of samurai cinema.

Kitano's reluctance to attempt a remake of *Zatoichi* is understandable to anyone familiar with its original star. Shintaro Katsu launched his screen career in 1954 with bit-parts for Daiei Studios. Far from the heights he would one day reach, his ambition at the time was simply to surpass Daiei rival Raizo Ichikawa. To do this, he remolded himself as an outlaw character actor, taking the role of blind super-villain in *Fushiranui Kengyo* (*Agent Kengyo*), a forerunner to his next on-screen creation - Zatoichi.

Katsu quickly became fascinated with his trademark character, finding inspiration all around him. His long-suffering wife, Tamao Nakamura, described him as obsessed. "He thought of movies 365 days of the year," she remarked after his death. The result was a new style of samurai flick, one which introduced an action-packed story that had for a hero an itinerant blind masseur with near-superhuman senses. Indeed, Katsu's on-screen antics gave rise to Zatoichi-kenpo, a novel school of swordplay. Furthermore, the *Zatoichi* series dispensed with the standard riverside swordfight scenes, bringing the action into town to create guerilla-style urban conflicts that have been mimicked ever since. Lone samurai dueling lone samurai was replaced with fight-scene confusion and the free-for-all realism of yakuza rumbles.

Through Katsu's determination to offer something radically different to what had come before, *Zatoichi* not only brought innovation to the genre, but also changed the way period dramas are perceived even today. Long before he had completed his 26th and last *Zatoichi* picture, Shintaro Katsu had become a household name and Japanese screen legend.

Katsu Shintaro Zatoichi Filmography

Zatoichi Monogatari
(1962, Daiei Kyoto)
Director: Kenji Misumi   96 min

Zoku Zatoichi Monogatari
(1962, Daiei Kyoto)
Director: Kazuo Mori   72 min

Shin Zatoichi Monogatari
(1963, Daiei Kyoto)
Director: Tokuzo Tanaka   91 min

Zatoichi Kyojo Tabi
(1963, Daiei Kyoto)
Director: Tokuzo Tanaka   86 min

Zatoichi Kenka Tabi
(1963, Daiei Kyoto)
Director: Kimiyoshi Yasuda   87 min

Zatoichi Senryo Kubi
(1964, Daiei Kyoto)
Director: Kazuo Ikehiro   82 min

Zatoichi Abare Dako
(1964, Daiei Kyoto)
Director: Kazuo Ikehiro   82 min

Zatoichi Kesho Tabi
(1964, Daiei Kyoto)
Director: Kenji Misumi   87 min

Zatoichi Sekisho Yaburi
(1964, Daiei Kyoto)
Director: Kimiyoshi Yasuda   86 min

Zatoichi Nidan Giri
(1965, Daiei Kyoto)
Director: Akira Inoue   83 min

Zatoichi Sakate Giri
(1965, Daiei Kyoto)
Director: Kazuo Mori   77 min

Zatoichi Jigoku Tabi
(1965, Daiei Kyoto)
Director: Kenji Misumi   87 min

Zatoichi no Utaga Kikoeru
(1966, Daiei Kyoto)
Director: Tokuzo Tanaka   83 min

Zatoichi Umi o Wataru
(1966, Daiei Kyoto)
Director: Kazuo Ikehiro   82 min

Zatoichi Tekka Tabi
(1967, Daiei Kyoto)
Director: Kimiyoshi Yasuda   93 min

Zatoichi Ro Yaburi
(1967, Katsu Pro, Daiei Kyoto)
Director: Satsuo Yamamoto   95 min

Zatoichi Chikemuri Kaido
(1967, Daiei Kyoto)
Director: Kenji Misumi   86 min

Zatoichi Hatashijo
(1968, Daiei Kyoto)
Director: Kimiyoshi Yasuda   82 min

Zatoichi Kenka Daiko
(1968, Daiei Kyoto)
Director: Kenji Misumi   82 min

Zatoichi to Yojimbo
(1970, Daiei Kyoto)
Director: Kihachi Okamoto   116 min

Zatoichi Abare Himatsuri
(1970, Katsu Pro, Daiei Kyoto)
Director: Kenji Misumi   95 min

Shin Zatoichi Yabure! Tojin Ken
(1971, Katsu Pro, Daiei Kyoto)
Director: Kimiyoshi Yasuda   95 min

Zatoichi Goyo Tabi
(1972, Katsu Pro)
Director: Kazuo Mori   90 min

Shin Zatoichi Monogatari Oreta Tsue
(1972, Katsu Pro)
Director: Shintaro Katsu   92 min

Shin Zatoichi Monogatari Kasama no Chimatsuri
(1973, Katsu Pro)
Director: Kimiyoshi Yasuda   88 min

Zatoichi
(1989, Katsu Pro)
Director: Shintaro Katsu   116 min

Tsubaki Sanjuro (1962, Toho, Kurosawa Production)
Sanjuro Tsubaki
Akira Kurosawa
Toshiro Mifune, Tatsuya Nakadai, Keiju Kobayashi
98 min

Poster (20 x 29 inch) $60.00

ご存じ三十郎
面白さ！
もの凄さ！
世界を唸らせた
逆抜き不意討ち斬り

黒沢 明
監督作品

椿三十郎

A delightfully amusing film originally made as a sequel to the famed *Yojimbo*, which itself was made into a Hollywood Western. The role of Sanjuro Tsubaki is played by none other than Toshiro Mifune. This time around he sides with a group of young samurai to expose the evil deeds of their boss, and with remarkable skill Mifune duels the baddie responsible for the confrontation. Mifune's swordplay in the film was said to be too fast for the camera to follow.

Yokachigozakura: Bajo no Wakamusha (1962, Toei Kyoto)
Yokachigozakura: Young Samurai Riders
Toshikazu Kono
Kinya Kitaoji, Jo Mizuki, Tetsuko Kobayashi

Poster (20 x 29 inch) $15.00

Daisan no Kagemusha (1963, Daiei Kyoto)
The Third Kagemusha
Umetsugu Inoue
Raizo Ichikawa, Hizuru Takachiho, Masayo Banri
104 min

Poster (20 x 29 inch) $80.00

At the dawn of the Meiji era, young warriors gather across the land to plot the downfall of the government. At Kyushu's Hitoyoshi Castle, Denhachiro Miyake and his trusty men take a stand. In order to aid his companions, who are now surrounded, Denhachiro makes a daredevil escape and rides off to deliver a message to the Satsuma army. Just when it looks like they're toast, reinforcements arrive. But Denhachiro's horse has been overlooked in all the action, and is now rider-less, dejected and alone...

A period drama about a stand-in who, as was the custom during the Era of Warring States, loses his life to protect his master. Raizo Ichikawa plays both Yasutaka Ikemoto, the brave lord of Mitani Castle, and Kyonosuke Ninomiya, his third *kagemusha*, whose fate, though cruel, is to be expected in such a profession.

Kogan Ittoryu (1963, Toei Kyoto)
Kogan Itto Sword Style
Shoji Matsumura
Hiroki Matsukata, Hiroko Sakuramachi, Yuriko Mishima

Poster (20 x 29 inch) $28.00

Set during the Era of the Warring States. Young Yagoro Itto of Izu's Oshima Island kills a man for violating his lover and is sent into exile. As he grows up, he becomes skilled in the martial arts. This worries the members of the Yagyu School, who believe his strength to be a threat, and they set out to get him. But in the all-out confrontation, Yagoro's mastery of the sword is exceptional, and with his victory he establishes the famous Ittoryu sword fighting style.

Poster (20 x 29 inch) $35.00

Mushuku was the term given to those Edo era unfortunates whose names were removed from family registers (*ninbetsucho*) for having committed crimes. Even after their terms of punishment had expired they were prohibited from returning to society. Instead, the shogunate forcibly sent them to mine gold on Sado Island for the sake of "maintaining the peace". The film depicts the mushuku uprising and eventual escape from the harsh treatment.

Roningai no Kaoyaku (1963, Toei Kyoto)
Boss of the Ronin Street
Yasushi Sasaki
Utaemon Ichikawa, Hizuru Takachiho, Kazuko Matsuo
86 min

Poster (20 x 29 inch) $80.00

Hanbei Tsukomo heads for the Suoya family store to help out the younger sister of his *ronin* friend. However, the Suoya brood has prospered nicely from selling the girl to a bureaucrat. Hanbei's interference is not well received, and the family soon hires the Hanya mob to put the squeeze on the townsfolk. Tempers flare as Hanbei and his ronin buddies take a stand.

Sengoku Yaro (1963, Toho)
Warring Clans
Kihachi Okamoto
Yuzo Kayama, Ichiro Nakaya, Makoto Sato
98 min

Poster (20 x 29 inch) $80.00

Young ninja Kittan wanders through enemy territory, and must defend himself from countless attacks by rival ninja. On his travels, he comes across a country samurai, who warns him of an approaching caravan of traders. Although such traders usually transport rice and salt, this time they're carrying weapons of mass destruction - *tanegashima* (matchlocks).

Teuchi (1963, Daiei Kyoto)
Death by Sword
Tokuzo Tanaka
Raizo Ichikawa, Yukiko Fuji, Kenzaburo Jo
85 min

Poster (20 x 29 inch) $80.00

The shogun's vassal Genjiro Shindo is forced to commit *seppuku* for daring to yawn. His fellow vassals are none too happy with this rather severe penalty and rise up against their masters. Forming a gang of underling toughs called the Shiratsuka Gang, they go in search of their former masters. However, the vassal Harima Aoyama is distressed by the state of affairs, and takes over the leadership of the gang in order to put a stop to the violence.

Shinsengumi Shimatsuki (1963, Daiei Kyoto)
Band of Assassins
Kenji Misumi
Raizo Ichikawa, Kenzaburo Jo, Shigeru Amachi
93 min

Poster (20 x 29 inch) $80.00

The story begins with *ronin* Tsubame Yamazaki, played by Raizo Ichikawa, joining Shinsengumi, a samurai band that boasts the revered warrior Kondo Isami as a member. Vice Captain Hijikata is miffed, believing Yamazaki's integrity will only lead to problems, and tries to dump him. But in the end, even the jaded Hijikata is won over.

Edo Hanzaicho: Kuroi Tsume (1964, Toei Kyoto)
Edo Crime Diaries: Black Nails
Kosaku Yamashita
Hiroki Matsukata, Nobuo Kaneko, Kou Nishimura
94 min

Poster (20 x 29 inch) $15.00

The bodies of three drowned sisters are found floating in Sumida River. Kantaro, a failed vassal but owner of a famed sword, falls under suspicion and is taken in for interrogation. However, the sword turns out to be a fake. The Magistrates Court quickly closes the case, ignoring the efforts of government official Mitsugu Tatara. What is behind the cover-up?

Bakuto-zamurai (1964, Daiei Kyoto)
Gambling Samurai
Kazuo Mori
Raizo Ichikawa, Kojiro Hongo, Mikiko Tsubochi
93 min

Poster (20 x 29 inch) $80.00

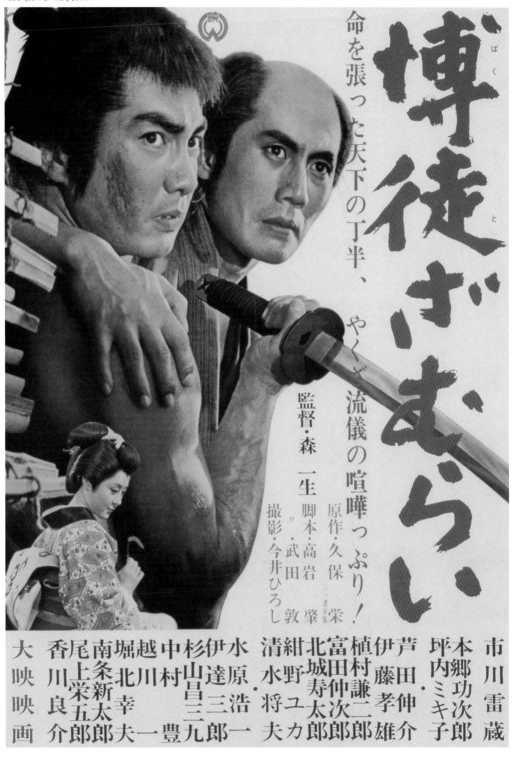

Drifter Sensoke Yuten becomes as famous as Ichien Koshu thanks to Bunkichi, retainer to the big boss Tsumugi. The Domoyasu family, which has long coveted Bunkichi's gambling den, gives him a good going over on some lame excuse. Senosuke kills the Domoyasu bodyguard, but as a result Bunkichi is banished to a far-off island as retribution.

Nemuri Kyoshiro: Engetsu Giri (1964, Daiei Kyoto)
The Exploits of Kyoshiro Nemuri, Swordsman
Kimiyoshi Yasuda
Raizo Ichikawa, Yuko Hamada, Kyoko Azuma
85 min

Poster (20 x 29 inch) $70.00

The third film in the popular series starring Raizo Ichikawa as the lovable killer and ladies man Kyoshiro Nemuri. With ambitions to be the next shogun, Takayuki Katagiri goes down to the river to try out his new sword. There he meets an old peasant fleeing the famine of his land. Katagiri slices him into little pieces. Just at that moment, Kyoshiro Nemuri is passing on the road above and sees what takes place. Katagiri, mistaking him for the peasant's friend, goes after him as well.

Nemuri Kyoshiro: Shobu (1964, Daiei Kyoto)
The Adventures of Kyoshiro Nemuri, Swordsman
Kenji Misumi
Raizo Ichikawa, Shiho Fujimura, Miwa Takada
83 min

Poster (20 x 29 inch) $120.00

Kyoshiro Nemuri meets by chance an old eccentric who turns out to be Iori Asahina, an accountant down at the Magistrates Court. Asahina's financial reform of the shogunate has made him many enemies, including followers of Takahime, the daughter of the shogun. Kyoshiro sympathizes with Asahina and takes up his sword to protect him. This second installment in the feature film series is said to be a masterpiece.

Kedamono no Ken (1965, Haiyuza)
The Monster's Sword
Hideo Gosha
Mikijiro Hira, Go Kato, Shima Iwashita
90 min

Poster (20 x 29 inch) $30.00

Gennosuke Hiraki, a nihilistic *ronin* who has been deceived by the chief retainers, kills the top retainer of the castle while his master is away in Edo, and is exiled. Misa, the daughter of the dead retainer, and Daisaburo Torio, her fiance, follow him to exact revenge.

Abare Go'uemon (1966, Toho)
Rough Go'uemon
Hiroshi Inagaki
Toshiro Mifune, Nobuko Otowa, Makoto Sato
100 min

Poster (20 x 58 inch) $80.00

Set during the Era of the Warring States.
Go'uemon is the horseback-riding chief of the
Kaga Shichi Gang, feared and notorious trou-
blemakers. While still kids, his two brothers
were snatched by a warlord and have been
kept since as hostages. The gang gets caught
up in a power struggle between despotic war-
lords, who treat them mercilessly, which is only
to be expected.

Jyoi Uchi: Hairyozuma Shimatsu (1967, Mifune Production, Toho)
Order of Attack
Masaki Kobayashi
Toshiro Mifune, Go Kato, Tatsuyoshi Ehara

Poster (20 x 29 inch) $80.00

Clan Samurai Isaburo Sasahara has been ordered to marry off his eldest son to
one of his master's mistresses. He isn't keen on the idea, but must obey his boss
and so gives his son away to Ichi, a wonderful woman by all accounts. The
newlyweds look set to live happily ever after. However, the clan suddenly orders
Ichi be returned to her former master. The story portrays the clan samurai who
resisted the inhumane feudalistic social system of the Edo period. The film won
the International Critics Association Award at the Venice Film Festival in 1967.

Poster (20 x 58 inch) $80.00

Hitori Okami (1968, Daiei Kyoto)
Lone Wolf
Ikehiro Kazuo
Raizo Ichikawa, Mayumi Ogawa, Kaneko Iwasaki
84 min

Isazo of Oiwake is a lonely, gang-less yakuza with a criminal record. However, he's respected by his fellow yakuza for his gambling and sword skills. But it's not enough for Isazo, who, haunted by his dark past, roams from one province to the next.

Akage (1969, Mifune Production)
Red Lion
Kihachi Okamoto
Toshiro Mifune, Minoru Terada, Etsushi Takahashi
116 min

Poster (20 x 29 inch) $80.00

Set at the end of the Edo period, the story follows redheaded Gonzo. Farmer-turned-soldier, Gonzo is recruited by Sekiho-tai, the vanguard of the Emperor's army that is marching on Edo. He is sent back to his hometown on a mission to save the imprisoned daughters of farmers unable to pay the feudal rice tax. Accomplishing his task, Gonzo next turns to the local governor, raiding his rice stores on behalf of the hungry farmers. He becomes a hero, much to the annoyance of the governor, who spreads the rumor that he's a fake and that the lord has been killed because of him.

"Samurai Banners"

Furinkazan (1969, Mifune Production)
Samurai Banners
Hiroshi Inagaki
Toshiro Mifune, Yoshiko Sakuma, Mayumi Ozora
165 min

Poster (20 x 29 inch) $70.00

A huge hit, this film describes the eventful life of Kansuke Yamamoto, an accomplished staff officer in the army of the Takeda Clan during the Warring States period, who's burning ambition was to unite Japan. Directed by the master of samurai dramas, Hiroshi Inagaki, and featuring top stars Toshiro Mifune, Kinnosuke Nakamura and Yujiro Ishihara. Emblazoned on the Takeda army's banners is *fu rin ka zan* (wind, forest, fire and mountain), a famous quote from Sun Tzu's *The Art of War*. It implies that the army should travel as fast as the wind but as quietly as a forest, invade like fire and be as immovable as a mountain.

Shinsengumi (1969, Mifune Production)
Shinsengumi
Tadashi Sawajima
Toshiro Mifune, Keiju Kobayashi, Kinya Kitaoji
165 min

Tenguto (1969, Daiei Kyoto)
Tengu-to
Satsuo Yamamoto
Tatsuya Nakadai, Fumiko Wakao, Go Kato
165 min

Poster (20 x 58 inch) $80.00

Poster (20 x 58 inch) $30.00

The second movie after *Akage* (Red Lion) by Mifune Productions, the independent film company established by Toshiro Mifune. It tells the story of Shinsengumi, the band of assassins that violently defended the shogunate against the forces that would ultimately overthrow it at the end of the Edo era. Laughably, they were also seen as a national police force. Toshiro Mifune plays Isami Kondo, Shinsengumi founder and leader.

Sentaro, a farmer forced to leave his village for not coming up with the land tax, flees to Edo, where he studies swordsmanship, turns to gambling, and eventually sets off back home. On the way, his sword skills come to the attention of Sentaro, commander of Tengu-to, a group formed to give foreigners a hard time, prop up the Emperor and generally make life tough for the little people. Sentaro is taken on as a hired sword. Tengu-to's activities take them far and wide, but the group is hampered by the appearance of a rival gang impersonating Tengu-to, but having a lot more fun.

Hiken Yaburi (1969, Daiei Kyoto)
Broken Swords
Kazuo Ikehiro
Hiroki Matsukata, Kojiro Hongo, Tomomi Iwai
■ 76 min

Oni no Sumu Yakata (1969, Daiei Kyoto)
The House of Demons
Kenji Misumi
Shintaro Katsu, Hideko Takamine, Michiyo Aratama
■ 76 min

Poster (20 x 29 inch) $20.00

Poster (20 x 29 inch) $20.00

A remake of Raizo Ichikawa's masterpiece *Samurai Vendetta* and offshoot of the much-used Chushingura story. The plot revolves around the friendship between two men and the tragedy of a married couple. Hiroki Matsukata reprises Raizo Ichikawa's role in this and the future *Kyoshiro Nemuri* series.

Taro flees the war and sets himself up as a thief. By day, he hides out in a desolate mountain temple with the beautiful Aizen. One day a monk turns up who seems to know all about Aizen, Taro, and his long-forgotten wife. The passions that Aizen induces in the two men lead to a calamitous and tragic ending.

1970~1989
昭和四十五年～平成元年

Ezoyakata no Ketto (1970, Toho)
The Final Battle at Ezo Manor
Kengo Furusawa
Yuzo Kayama, Rentaro Mikuni, Mitsuko Baisho
131 min

Poster (20 x 29 inch) $40.00

Eight men head for Hakodate on Japan's northern island of Hokkaido. Their mission is to rescue Walsa, the daughter of a Russian count kidnapped by Jirozaemon, the lord of Ezo Manor. But little do they know that their master is using them to lay his evil hands on money and weapons.

Machibuse (1970, Mifune Production)
Ambush
Hiroshi Inagaki
Toshiro Mifune, Yujiro Ishihara, Shintaro Katsu
117 min

Poster (20 x 29 inch) $60.00

Five strangers arrive at the Toge Teahouse. As their backgrounds are revealed, so is their plot to relieve the local clan of its riches. Tozaburo Shinogi, a *ronin* who occasionally does spy work, receives an order to assassinate a man whom he believes to be his friend.

Kogarashi Monjiro: Kakawari Gozansen (1972, Toei Kyoto)
Cold Country Wind Monjiro: Kakawari Gozansen
Sadao Nakajima
Bunta Sugawara, Kunie Tanaka, Eiko Nakamura
90 min

Poster (20 x 29 inch) $20.00

Tsunehei of Hachiman is all smiles after Monjiro saves his life. He introduces Monjiro to Omitsu, a friend of the prostitute Okoma, who Tsunehei has his eye on. But Monjiro is a little shaken when he hears Omitsu singing to herself while drunk, and asks her about her background. It turns out that Omitsu is his long-lost sister, from whom he was separated in childhood.

Goyokiba (1972, Toho)
Sword of Justice
Kenji Misumi
Shintaro Katsu, Yukiji Asaoka, Mari Atsumi
108 min

Poster (20 x 29 inch) $25.00

Goyokiba: Kamisori Hanzo Jigokuzeme (1973, Toho)
Razor 2: The Snare
Yasuzo Masumura
Shintaro Katsu, Kou Nishimura, Hosei Komatsu
89 min

Poster (20 x 29 inch) $55.00

The film version of the weekly comic series of the same name. This is the first of three films that depict the nefarious activities of one Hanzo Itami, aka "Hanzo the Razor", a low ranking cop at the northern district Magistrates Court, who breaks all the rules of community policing. His unique sense of justice includes using sex and torture to plumb the criminal depths of society

Second in the "Hanzo the Razor" series. Hanzo, the unorthodox cop, hears from a thief he's nabbed about a murder involving *ko'oroshi* (abortion) practiced at the local shrines and temples. He breaks into a shrine outside of his jurisdiction, tortures a priestess, and reveals the truth about a prostitution racket run by the convent. Must be seen to be believed!

Poster (20 x 58 inch) $45.00

Miyamoto Musashi (1973, Shochiku Ofuna)
Musashi Miyamoto
Tai Kato
Hideki Takahashi, Jiro Tamiya, Keiko Matsuzaka
148 min

The story of Musashi Miyamoto, master swordsman of the Warring States period. Although numerous film adaptations exist, this *chanbara* version focuses on Musashi's youth. It tells the story of his single-minded pursuit to master the sword through to his famous duel with rival Kojiro Sasaki on Ganryu Island.

Mushukunin Mikogami no Jokichi: Tasogare ni Senko ga Tonda (1973, Toho)
Mushukunin Mikogami no Jokichi: Tasogare ni Senko ga Tonda
Kazuo Ikehiro
Yoshio Harada, Isao Natsuyagi, Michiyo Yasuda
83 min

Poster (20 x 29 inch) $20.00

Last in the series of three films about lone wolf yakuza Jokichi of Mikogami, who wanders the entire country looking to avenge the cruel murder of his wife and children. This "wandering gambler" action movie was produced by Toho following the success of the *Kogarashi Monijiro* television series. Jokichi develops a peculiar friendship when he exchanges swords with an assassin whom he meets while traveling, little knowing that the assassin has been sent by his enemy to kill him.

Okita Soshi (1974, Toho Eiga)
Soshi Okita
Masanobu Deme
Masao Kusakari, Kyoko Mano, Shino Ikenami
92 min

Poster (20 x 29 inch) $10.00

The story takes place during the last turbulent days of the Edo era. Soshi Okita is a member of the notorious Shinsengumi, and single-mindedly follows The Way of the Sword, eating dirt and swallowing the hardships of the lifestyle he has chosen. The film ends with his death at the tragically young age of twenty-five.

Okami yo Rakujitsu o Kire Fu'un Hen, Gekijo Hen, Doto Hen (1974, Shochiku Ofuna)
The Last Samurai: Wind and Clouds, Passion and Angry Waves
Kenji Misumi
Hideki Takahashi, Keiko Matsuzaka, Ken Ogata
159 min

Poster (20 x 29 inch) $20.00

This film portrays the lives of two young men, Toranosuke Sugi and Hanjiro Nakamura, amidst the confusion of the waning Edo period. While having mutually opposing views, they accept each other through their respect for The Way of the Sword and become close buddies. A long, rambling period drama, it depicts the vivid way of life, and death, of the master swordsmen and the few that survived the bloodshed.

Women of the Sword: Uma vs. Japan

Quentin Tarantino's geeky adulation of Asian cinema is no secret. In his most recent production, *Kill Bill*, the steady stream of elements snatched from samurai and *chanbara* movies is unmistakable to anyone with even a passing interest in the genre. But it is his lead, Uma Thurman, who really drives the message home. In her role as the Bride, a samurai-sword wielding sociopath, she has revised and reinvented the role of *onna kenshi* for a 21st century audience. Finally, it would seem, the lady samurai has made it to Hollywood.

However, as we watch Ms. Thurman grunt her way through near two hours of on-screen mass murder with little more threatening than a blade and a banana-yellow jogging suit, it becomes impossible to avoid the yet-to-be-asked question: In an industry that at its peak was churning out a movie a week, where are Japan's Women of the Sword?

The answer, like so much pertaining to Japan's fairer sex, is multi-layered. On one level we have *Azumi* (2003), the story of a 17th century ninja-raised assassin, who, with her fellow acolytes, is dispatched on one mission after another

Azumi (2003, Azumi Committee)
Director: Ryuhei Kitamura
142 min

to rid the Tokugawa government of real and imagined enemies. The eponymous Azumi, played by Aya Ueto, has the two essential ingredients by which to guarantee transgender success at today's box office. Ueto is impossibly cute, with pouting, bee-stung lips and a schoolgirl air of innocence. But Azumi can also kick ass. In the film's climactic ending, the 18-year old manages to thrust, slash and gouge her way through 200 nasty-looking samurai, leaving a body-count that would warm even the cockles of Tarantino's jaded heart.

Preceding Azumi, but working the same formula, was *Princess Blade* (*Shirayuki-Hime*) (2001), which had another ridiculously lovable teenager, in this case played by Yumiko Shaku, take up the good sword. *Princess* differs however in that it takes place in the future and follows Yuki, the daughter of assassins, as she hunts down the killers of her dear but murderous mother. Donnie Yen, that famed Hong Kong martial artist and, more recently, choreographer for *Blade 2*, is responsible for Yumiko's high-flying frolicking.

Shurayuki-Hime (2001, Shurayuki-Hime Production Committee)
Director: Shunsuke Sato
92 min

Hana no Oedo no Yakuzahime (1961, Toei Kyoto)
Director: Eiichi Kudo
87 min

Hibari no Utamatsuri Furisode Torimonocho
(1953, Shochiku Kyoto)
Director: Torajiro Saito

Turning the clock back, it is necessary to do a little barrel-bottom scraping if we are to find anything that can be likened to *Kill Bill*'s protagonist. In the golden age of the samurai flick, a woman's place was more often than not where the villain hope to have her and the hero whence to rescue her. For the cinema-going public, this was just how it should be. Few screenplays allowed their female roles to have a direct hand in the glinting-steel action unless, of course, they had something else to bring to the table.

One star who did was Misora Hibari, whose superstardom as a post-war songstress gave her the requisite muscle to choose and reshape her many period drama roles. Hibari appeared in a total of 158 films, a staggering 63 of those made in the five years between 1957 and 1961. At a time when a movie a month was the norm, the work schedule that such actors as Hibari accepted with barely a flicker of the eyelash would have the likes of today's Thurman begging for a swift, clean end to it all.

Hibari no Mori no Ishimatsu (1960, Toei Kyoto)
Director: Tadashi Sawashima
83 min

On another, and quite separate level, there is *Samurai Girl 21* (2001). Not a genre classic in its own right, but certainly a favorite down at the video store, this straight-to-DVD-with-accompanying-photo-book stars none other that TV's large-breasted doyenne Eiko Koike. As the title implies, Koike does appear occasionally with sword in hand. However, she tends to spend more time in swimsuit alongside a legion of equally well-

stacked bimbos talking nonsense and negotiating a number of unnatural body positions. Admittedly, she does put herself to risk when she appears at a cabaret club heckled by drunk salary men baying for naked flesh. Furthermore, she could beat Uma hands-down in a wet T-shirt contest.

Samurai Girl 21 (2001, Samurai Girl 21 Committee)
Director: Ataru Oikawa
160 min

Hitogoroshi (1976, Nagata Production, Daiei Eiga, Eizou Kyoto)
Killer
Yusaku Matsuda, Yoko Takahashi, Junko Igarashi
82 min

Poster (20 x 29 inch) $70.00

Ako-Jo Danzetsu (1978, Toei Kyoto, Toei Uzumasa Eigamura)
The Fall of Ako Castle
Kinji Fukasaku
Kinnosuke Yorozuya, Hideo Shimazu, Takuya Fujioka
140 min

Poster (20 x 29 inch) $10.00

Rokube Futago, the most cowardly member of his clan, is officially ordered to do the job no one else wants. He must avenge his lord by killing Koken Nito, the man that everyone most fears. To achieve his goal, Rokube develops a unique and inexplicable method. Arriving at the inn before his target, he yells from a safe distance, "That man is a murderer! No one knows when he might kill again!" This supposedly does the trick...

Set in the fourteenth year of the Genroku period, it is yet another film version of the Chushingura incident, in which the 47 *ronin* of Ako invade the house of Kira. This story continues to be told as one of the classic romantic folk legends of Japan, and has given rise to many famous works in a variety of media, including novels, plays and movies. This is the twenty-fifth film based on Chushingura. Sonny Chiba, of *Kill Bill* fame, stars as ronin Kazuemon Fuwa.

Kumokiri Nizaemon (1978, Shochiku, Haiyuza)
Bandits vs. Samurai Squad
Hideo Gosha
Tatsuya Nakadai, Somegoro Ichikawa, Koshiro Matsumoto
160 min

Poster (20 x 29 inch) $10.00

Mito Komon (1978, Toei Kyoto)
Mito Komon
Tetsuya Yamauchi
Eijiro Tono, Kotaro Satomi, Shinya Owada
88 min

Poster (20 x 29 inch) $10.00

Nizaemon Kumokiri, out for revenge after being framed for a crime that never happened, becomes a Japanese Robin Hood, stealing only from wealthy merchants with the motto: "I don't rape, don't kill, and don't rob from the poor". Troublemaker Shikibu Abe, a former thief and now governor, is not amused, and challenges Nizaemon to a fight to the death.

A film of undisguised poetic justice. Mitsukuni Mito, vice shogun of the entire country, disguises himself and travels through the land with his loyal retainer, righting wrongs and dealing severely with anyone who makes life a misery for the common folk. This is the 17th Toei picture on the theme, and includes the cast from the popular television series.

Sanada Yukimura no Boryaku (1979, Toei Kyoto)
The Shogun Assassins
Sadao Nakajima
Hiroki Matsukata, Kinnosuke Yorozuya, Ichiro Ogura
148 min

Flyer (7 x 10 inch) $3.00

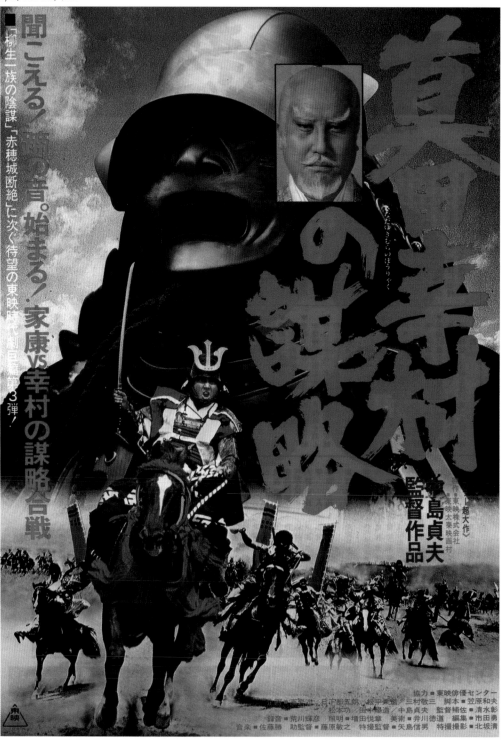

Yukimura Sanada, who was defeated at the famous Battle of Sekigahara, wants Ieyasu Tokugawa's head. Tokugawa, in turn, wants to achieve his ambition of uniting the entire country. Yukimura cooks up numerous schemes together with his "Ten Brave Men" - specially trained combat troops - but Ieyasu gets wind of Yukimura's plans, and sends his ninja troops, led by Hanzo Hattori, to meet him.

Chanbara Graffiti Kiru! (1981, Toei Kyoto)
The Chanbara Graffiti
Toshiro Uratani
Matsunosuke Onoue, Chiezo Kataoka, Utaemon Ichikawa
96 min

Poster (20 x 29 inch) $25.00

Commemorating the 30th anniversary of the founding of Toei Studios, this film comprises famous scenes from the most popular 100 movies chosen from among the 800 period dramas produced by Toei between the years 1951 and 1960. Successive generations of stars relive their memories of the era, including Chiezo Kataoka, Utaemon Ichikawa, Kinnosuke Yorozuya and Hashizo Okawa.

Shikakenin Baian (1981, Toei Kyoto)
Shikakenin Baian
Yasuo Furuhata
Kinnosuke Yorozuya, Katsuo Nakamura, Juzo Itami
100 min

Poster (20 x 29 inch) $7.00

Jirocho Seishun Hen: Tsuppari Shimizuko (1982, Shochiku)
Jirocho Seishun Hen: Tsuppari Shimizuko
Yoichi Maeda
Masatoshi Nakamura, Koichi Sato, Daijiro Harada
91 min

Poster (20 x 29 inch) $20.00

By day, a respected acupuncture therapist about town. By night, a hired killer. This is the life of Baian Fujieda. Chikaranosuke, eldest son of Nagatonokami Abe, retainer to the shogun, has violently murdered a housemaid. Nagatonokami, concerned for his own future, hires the services of Baian.

On the day his mother dies, young gambler Jirocho swears in front of her grave that he'll never gamble again. But, that night, Jirocho heads to a gambling den, where he bets the condolence money for his mother's funeral. No surprise to learn he loses the lot. Not the hard-boiled yakuza story it seems, this is a comedy featuring many new artists who were making a name for themselves at the time.

Ran (1985, Herald Ace, Greenwich Film Production)
Ran
Akira Kurosawa
Tatsuya Nakadai, Satoshi Terao, Jinpachi Nezu
162 min

Flyer (7 x 10 inch) $1.00

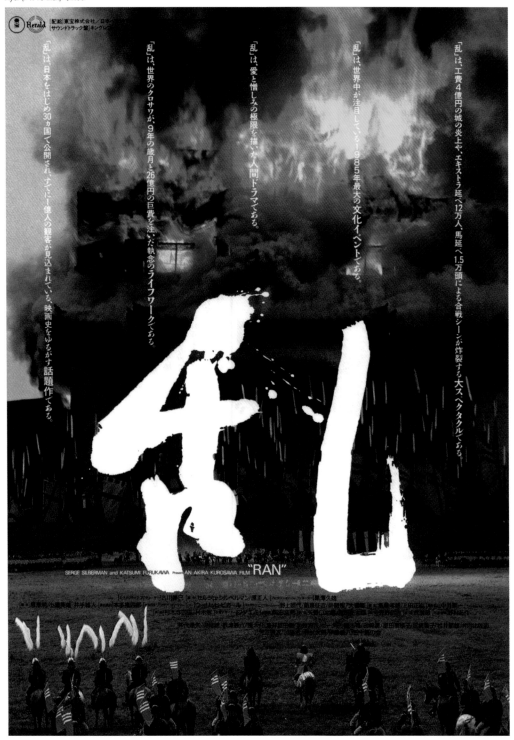

Based on *King Lear*, one of the four Shakespearean tragedies, this Warring States period epic is by world-famous director Kurosawa. The film is basically a montage of episodes featuring feudal warlord Motonari Mouri and his two brothers. The movie received Best Director, Best Art Direction and Best Cinematography nominations at the 1985 Academy Awards, and won Best Costume Design Award.

Chikamatsu Monzaemon: Yari no Gonza (1986, Shochiku, Hyogensha)
Monzaemon Chikamatsu: Gonza the Spearman
Masahiro Shinoda
Hiromi Go, Shima Iwashita, Shohei Hino
126 min

Poster (20 x 29 inch) $10.00

Hissatsu! (1984, Shochiku, Asahi Broadcasting Corporation)
Hissatsu!
Masahisa Sadanaga
Makoto Fujita, Isuzu Yamada, Kiyoshi Nakajo
124 min

Poster (20 x 29 inch) $15.00

Based on Monzaemon Chikamatsu's *joruri* traditional puppet play. Gonza Sasano is a young talented servant from Matsue Province. He serves food at ceremonies, does odd jobs, is good-looking, skilled with the spear, and can even perform tea ceremonies. He begs Osai, the wife of his tea master, to initiate him into the secrets of The Way of the Tea. However, he winds up being falsely accused of trying it on with the girl, and is forced into exile.

Hissatsu Shigotonin is a band of altruistic contract killers hired by commoners to settle grudges. The film commemorates the 600th episode of the popular *Hissatsu Shigotonin* TV series. Hissatsu members, which include Mondo Nakamura, a low level cop, Okuri, a *shamisen* player, Hide, a hairpin maker, and Kayo, a jack-of-all-trades, knock off one baddie after another with their specialized killing skills.

Ryoma o Kitta Otoko (1987, Armance Planning)
The Man who Killed Ryoma
Kosaku Yamashita
Kenichi Hagiwara, Miwako Fujitani, Jinpachi Nezu
109 min

Poster (20 x 29 inch) $10.00

The film describes the short life of Tadasaburo Sasaki, a terrorist who took the life of famous revolutionary Ryoma Sakamoto at the end of the Edo era. The actor portraying Tadasaburo is Kenichi Hagiwara, previously a popular vocalist in the rock group, The Tempters. Co-star Miwako Fujitani recently caused a ruckus by trying to enter Tokyo's Imperial Palace under the pretext that she was related to the crown princess. Her face does resemble the crown princess...slightly.

Shogun Iemitsu no Ranshin Gekitotsu (1989, Toei Kyoto)
The Madness of Shogun Iemitsu, Gekitotsu (Crash)
Yasuo Furuhata
Ken Ogata, Ippei Shigeyama, Shinichi Chiba
110 min

Flyer (7 x 10 inch) $1.00

The third shogun, Iemitsu, hates his eldest son Takechiyo because he doesn't resemble him. However, he treats his second son Tokumatsu with blind affection. Concerned about his waning chances of succession, Takechiyo sends assassins to kill Tokumatsu. However, Tokumatsu has seven serious bodyguards who whisk him off to Edo, risking their own lives in the process.

1990~2003
平成二年～平成十五年

Ten to Chi to (1990, Kadokawa Haruki Office)
Heaven and Earth
Haruki Kadokawa
Takaaki Enomoto, Masahiko Tsugawa, Atsuko Asano
118 min

Flyer (7 x 10 inch) $1.00

A grand Warring States period epic shot on the great plains of Canada. Climaxing with the famous Battle of Kawanakajima between Kenshin Uesugi and Shingen Takeda, the film explores the complex relationships between the main characters. The absurdly high production cost (for the time) of 5 billion yen captured the attention of the public, but rumors had it that at least half went on promotional fees. The movie blurb was "The first real spectacle since Ben Hur".

Edo-Jo Tairan (1991, Toei, Fuji Television)
The Edo Castle Rebellion
Toshio Masuda
Hiroki Matsukata, Yukiyo Toake, Shinobu Sakagami
113 min

Flyer (7 x 10 inch) $1.00

An entertaining samurai drama that depicts the conflicts that swirl around the fifth Tokugawa shogun at Edo Castle. The fourth shogun is nearing his death, but has no heir to take his place. Utanokami Sakai, the chief retainer, must prepare for the succession. However, Tsunashige, one of the candidates and younger brother of the shogun, is assassinated.

Kozure Okami: Sono Chiisaki Te ni (1993, Koike Kazuo Office)
Lone Wolf and Cub
Akira Inoue
Masakazu Tamura, Tatsuya Nakadai, Yuko Kotegawa
119 min

Flyer (7 x 10 inch) $1.00

Shiju-shichi Nin no Shikaku (1994, Toho Eiga)
47 Assassins
Kon Ichikawa
Ken Takakura, Kiichi Nakai, Hisaya Morishige
129 min

Flyer (7 x 10 inch) $1.00

Itto Ogami is official executioner of those feudal lords and their families convicted of crimes. But when his wife is killed in a plot engineered by the Yagyu Clan, he loses his cushy job. He swears revenge, and leaves with his son on a long journey. Although a well-known story, this samurai version differs from former remakes in that it highlights the relationship between father and son, and focuses less on swordplay. This was done at the request of Kazuo Koike, the writer of the original story.

Another Chushingura movie, this time focusing on the character of Kuranosuke Oishe. It tells the story of the maneuvering that took place between Kuranosuke, Matashiro Irobe and the Houses of Kira & Uesugi. The film was based on a best-selling novel, which introduced the concept of "economic war" into the story.

East Meets West (1995, Shochiku, Feature Film Enterprise, Kihachi Production)
East Meets West
Kihachi Okamoto
Hiroyuki Sanada, Ittoku Kishibe, Naoto Takenaka
124 min

Poster (20 x 29 inch) $18.00

This samurai cum cowboy comedy takes place in the American West of 1860. A shipment of gold coins, the bulk of a secret fund headed for the Japan-USA Friendship Delegation in San Francisco, has been stolen. The director, Kihachi Okamoto, wrote the first draft of the script a decade before he could finally fulfill his dream of turning it into a movie. Shot almost entirely on location in the United States.

SF Samurai Fiction (1998, SF Committee)
SF Samurai Fiction
Hiroyuki Nakano
Morio Kazama, Mitsuru Fukikoshi, Tomoyasu Hotei
111 min

Flyer (7 x 10 inch) $1.00

A new-style period drama depicting the adventures of a young samurai who tries to regain a precious sword stolen by a master swordsman *ronin*, but instead comes up against a middle-aged pacifist samurai. Hiroyuki Nakano, the director and screenwriter, is known as the "Kurosawa of Music Videos".

Yagyu Gaiden: Kunoichi Ninpocho
(1998, King Records, Marubeni, Tohokushinsha)
Biography of Yagyu: The Way of the Woman Ninja
Hitoshi Ozawa
Hitoshi Ozawa, Yuko Moriyama, Tomoro Taguchi
74 min

Flyer (7 x 10 inch) $1.00

The depraved lord Akinari Kato uses his band of assassins, who employ super-human ninjutsu, to snatch beautiful women for his all-night jaunts. When his gang brutally kills the family of Mondo Hori, the minister of justice, the seven surviving women commit themselves to revenge, adding a bit of their own ninja into the mix with the help of Jubei Yagyu, the famed swordsman.

Fukuro no Shiro (1999, Owls' Castle Committee)
Owls' Castle
Masahiro Shinoda
Kiichi Nakai, Mayu Tsuruta, Riona Hazuki
138 min

Flyer (7 x 10 inch) $1.00

The story of a fierce battle that rages between Juzo Tsuzura, one of the last Iga ninja and enemy of Hideyoshi Toyotomi, and Gohei Kazama, a ninja-turned-samurai. Includes steamy love affairs with two ninja babes.

Gohatto (1999, Shochiku, Kadokawa Shoten Publishing, IMAGICA, BS Asahi, Eisei Gekijo)
Taboo
Nagisa Oshima
Beat Takeshi, Ryuhei Matsuda, Shinji Takeda
100 min

Poster (29 x 40 inch) $20.00

Kyoto, at the end of Edo period. Sozaburo Kano, a beautiful youth, joins Shinsengumi, the band of assassins at the height of its power. However, all is not well. The other members grow jealous amid rumors of Sozaburo's homosexuality. Ryuhei Matsuda, son of Yusaku Matsuda of *Black Rain* fame, makes his screen debut in the lead role.

Gojoe Reisenki (2000, Suncent Cinema Works)
Gojoe
Sogo Ishi
Tadanobu Asano, Masatoshi Nagase, Daisuke Ryu
137 min

Flyer (7 x 10 inch) $1.00

The last years of the Heian period were a dark and savage time ruled by the Heike Clan. In Kyoto, more than 1000 Heike samurai are attacked one after another by what is believed to be a monster. However, the creature turns out to be none other than Yoshitsune Minamoto, a Genji Clan survivor who has mastered The Way of the Sword to revenge his fallen brethren. Benkei Musashibo, the apostate priest, receives word from God, of all people, that he's to "defeat the ogre". He sets out to do just that...

Anime: The New Type Samurai

In a medium that is big on theatrics, costume and combat, the samurai is made to be animated. It's not surprising then that we find him in some of anime's most successful productions, from Kenshin Himura in *Samurai X* and Inu-yasha in the film of the same name, to Rolonoa Zoror in *One Piece* and Goemon Ishikawa in *Lupin III*. He may turn to magic to battle his foes, but the trusty sword is never far from reach. The "ka-ching, ka-ching, phwut, aaaagh" as one head after another is lopped off is, without doubt, so much more compelling than the simple "bang, bang, your dead" of lesser characters. Game

makers certainly think so. Tidus and Auran in *Final Fantasy* and *FF-X2*'s Yuna, who keeps a samurai costume stashed in her closet, are all sword-wielding recreations from Japan's violent past. *Samurai Spirits* (aka *Samurai Shodown*) is everything it suggests.

Today's TV period dramas may be fodder for an older generation nostalgic for a cinematic era long since passed, but the samurai effect, if you like, is persistent, and looks set to continue long into the future.

Inu-yasha: Tha Fantasy Castle Within the Mirror (2002, Toho)
Director: Toshiya Shinohara
99 min

Inu-yasha: Love that Transcends Time (2001, Toho)
Director: Toshiya Shinohara
100 min

Kamui no Ken (1985, Toei)
Director: Rintaro
132 min

Kyuubi no Kitsune to Tobimaru
(1968, Daiei)
Director: Gentaro Nakajima
81 min

Rurouni Kenshin: Meiji Kenkaku
Romantan: Ishin Shishi he no
Requiem (1997, Sony Pictures
Entertainment)
Director: Hatsuki Tsuji
90 min

Ame Agaru (2000, Ame Agaru Committee)
Ame Agaru
Takashi Koizumi
Terao Akira, Yoshiko Miyazaki, Toshiro Mifune
91 min

Flyer (7 x 10 inch) $1.00

Akira Kurosawa worked on the screenplay of this movie right up until his death in 1998. A heartwarming story of a sword master whose modesty stands in the way of him being promoted. His wife sticks by him anyway. Directed by Takashi Koizumi, Kurosawa's assistant director for 28 years.

Azumi (2003, Azumi Committee)
Azumi
Ryuhei Kitamura
Aya Ueto, Joe Odagiri, Naoto Takenaka
142 min

Flyer (7 x 10 inch) $1.00

Based on a best-selling comic. Deep in the mountains, 10 children are raised to become assassins, but are forced to kill each other before undertaking their first task. The surviving five, including Azumi, are sent on a mission to assassinate those who are plotting against the Tokugawa shogunate. The final scene, in which 200 people are killed, is the mother of all slashfests.

Dora Heita (2000, Doraheita Committee)
Dora Heita
Kon Ichikawa
Koji Yakusho, Ryudo Uzaki, Bunta Sugawara
111 min

Flyer (7 x 10 inch) $1.00

A period action comedy centering around the exploits of newly appointed city magistrate Koheita Mochizuki as he attempts to clean up the corruption that surrounds him. Though the film, which was shown at the 50th Berlin International Film Festival (2000), was directed by Kon Ichikawa, the original story was written by all four members of Shiki no Kai: movie big guns Ichikawa, Akira Kurosawa, Keisuke Kinoshite and Masaki Kobayashi.

Red Shadow Akakage (2001, Red Shadow Akakage Committee)
Red Shadow Akakage
Hiroyuki Nakano
Masanobu Ando, Megumi Okina, Kumiko Aso
108 min

Flyer (7 x 10 inch) $1.00

Remake of the popular '60s ninja action TV series *Kamen no Ninja Akakage* set in the turbulent Japan of 1545. Sworn to the cause of national unification, Shirokage leads his band of cutthroat ninja on yet another mission improbable. This visually powerful movie attempted to depict the timeworn ninja story from a novel perspective, showing the masked assassins and their shadowy world in a new and engaging light.

Sukedatiya Sukeroku (2002, Nikkatsu, Fuji Television)
Sukeroku: The Protector
Kihachi Okamoto
Hiroyuki Sanada, Kyoka Suzuki, Tatsuya Nakadai
88 min

Flyer (7 x 10 inch) $1.00

Sukeroku is on his way home to Edo, when he comes across a dispute that quickly turns ugly. Unable to mind his own business, he draws his sword and saves the injured party from further injury. This sudden attack of altruism gives him an unexpected rush, and from that day forth he becomes Sukeroku: The Protector. One day he meets a samurai in distress who, unbeknownst to him, is in fact his own father. Super Sukeroku steps in to wield his sword...

"Twilight Samurai"

Tasogare Seibei (2002, Shochiku, Nippon Television Network, Sumitomo Corporation, Hakuhodo, Nippan, Eisei Gekijo)
Old Man Seibei
Yoji Yamada
Hiroyuki Sanada, Rie Miyazawa, Nenji Kobayashi
129 min

Flyer (7 x 10 inch) $1.00

It is the end of the Edo era, and Seibe Iguchi, a rank-and-file samurai from Shonai, has lost the taste for battle. His wife is dead and he has two daughters and an aged mother to look after. He sets his heart on going home, much to the disdain of his fellow warriors, who nickname him "Old Man Seibe". However, just when his career looks to hit bottom, his childhood friend Tomoe comes under attack, forcing Seibe into action. With this unexpected bloodletting, the "samurai spirit" is revived, and he happily heeds the call and marches off to battle.

Mibu Gishiden (2003, Mibu Gishiden Project)
The Legend of the Mibu Retainer
Yojiro Takita
Kiichi Nakai, Koichi Sato, Yui Natsukawa
137 minn

Flyer (7 x 10 inch) $1.00

Shinsengumi, that band of suicidal assassins desperately trying to prop up the doomed Tokugawa shogunate, has one member who stands apart from his fellow samurai. Kanchiro Yoshimura likes his money as much as the next man, but doesn't want to die for it. To him, family always comes first.

Makai Tensho (2003, Makai Tensho Committee)
From the Spirit World
Hideyuki Hirayama
Yosuke Kubozuka, Kumiko Aso, Koichi Sato
105 min

Flyer (7 x 10 inch) $1.00

Ganryujima (2003, Ganryujima Committee)
Ganryu Island
Seiji Chiba
Masahiro Motoki, Atsushi Tamura, Masahiko Nishimura
75 min

Flyer (7 x 10 inch) $1.00

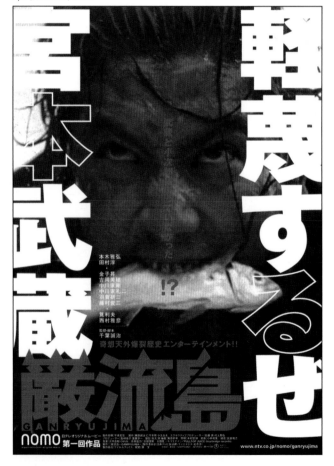

Based on the true story of the Shimabara Massacre. In 1638, in an attempt to stem the spread of the newly imported *Kirishitan* (Christian) religion, the Bakufu government carries out a mass slaughter of believers. Shiro Amakura, their leader, is one of the thousands murdered. Many years pass, and then one day Shiro returns from the dead, a resurrected corpse hungry for revenge. With him he brings an army of once illustrious samurai, upon whom he has bestowed a second life. In exchange, they must join him in his campaign to destroy Tokugawa. But master swordsman Jubei Yagyu catches wind of the evil plot and is determined to stop them.

Another story about legendary swordsman Musashi Miyamoto. Based on the much-told fight against enemy samurai Kojiro Sasaki and the "Final Fight on Ganryu Island", this film introduces a very new hypothesis to what is believed to be an established fact - that Musashi kicked Kojiro's ass!

Zatoichi (2003, Bandai Visual, Tokyo FM, Dentsu, Asahi National Broadcasting, Saito Entertainment, Office Kitano)
Zatoichi
Takeshi Kitano
Beat Takeshi, Tadanobu Asano, Michiyo Okusu
115 min

Flyer (7 x 10 inch) $1.00

Ichi, the staff-wielding blind masseur, turns up in a posting station where the unscrupulous Ginzo Gang rule big. The character of Zatoichi is resurrected with inimitable style by Takeshi Kitano, known in Japan as comedian Beat Takeshi, who manages to fill this classic tale with an extraordinary mix of action, comedy and music to create a *rakugo* drama quite unlike any other.

Samurai Souvenirs
Movie Memorabilia From a More Innocent Age

Of the memorabilia that samurai movies have spawned, afacionados point to *chirashi*, or flyers, as the most coveted items. More than simply printed sheets, the flyers for many of the films in this book were similar to the programs of today - small booklets that carried staff and cast listings, brief story synopses and highlights from the movies. Bought as souvenirs for 50 or 100 yen, many of these flyers now exchange hands for hundreds of dollars.

Sanjuro (1962, Toho, Kurosawa Production)
Tsubaki Sanjuro $180.00

Yojimbo (1961, Toho, Kurosawa Production)
Yojimbo $400.00

Kakushi Toride no San Akunin (1958, Toho)
The Hidden Fortress $200.00

Kumonosu-Jo (1957, Toho)
Throne of Blood $200.00

Shichinin no Samurai (1954, Toho)
Seven Samurai $200.00

Shin-Heike Monogatari (1955, Daiei Kyoto)
$80.00

Tange Zazen: Kokezaru no Tsubo
(1955, Daiei Kyoto) $150.00

INDEX

INDEX

Romanized Titles